****************MEDICAL MEDIUM****************

THYROID HEALING

Diet

COOKBOOK

Life-changing Diet Recipes to Rescue the Thyroid and Bring You Back to Health and Vitality.

By

Brain Thompson

****************MEDICAL MEDIUM*****************

Copyright © 2019, By: Brain Thompson

ISBN-13: 978-1-950772-36-0
ISBN-10: 1-950772-36-5

All Rights Reserved. No part of this publication may be reproduced in any form or by any means, including scanning, photocopying, or otherwise without prior written permission of the copyright holder.

Disclaimer:

The information provided in this book is designed to provide helpful information on the subjects discussed. The publisher and author are not responsible for any specific health or allergy needs that may require medical supervision and are not liable for any damages or negative consequences from any treatment, action, application or preparation, to any person reading or following the information in this book.

****************MEDICAL MEDIUM****************

Table of Contents

Introductions: 8

    It Time for You to Take Control and Become a True Thyroid Expert 8

        Causes of Hashimoto's Disease? 9

        Symptoms of the Hashimoto's disease? 9

        Treatment of Hashimoto's Disease 10

        Complications related to Hashimoto 11

Diet Recipes to Help You Take Control of your Health and Become a True Thyroid Expert 12

    Thyroid Healing Delectable Breakfast Recipes 12

        Farmer's Wife Sunday Breakfast 12

        Balancing Pumpkin Smoothie 14

        Warming Amaranth Porridge 15

        Oyster Pancake as Thyroid Diet Foods 17

        Egg-free Gluten-free Pancake 19

        Paleo Wild Blueberry Bagels 20

        Baked Stuffed Pumpkin 22

        Braised Green Cabbage 23

        Steamed Collard Greens 24

        Roasted Brussel Sprouts and Grapes 25

        Salmon Goes Dancing with Salsa Verde 26

        Easy Thai Salmon 27

    Wild Blueberry Apple Spiced Slow Cooker Oats 29

        Wild Blueberry, Cranberry and Almond Oatmeal 30

        Dried Wild Blueberry and Almond Granola 31

        Wild Blueberry Protein Smoothie 32

        Coconut Peanut Butter Wild Blueberry Toast 33

        Paleo, raw, gluten free, dairy free 34

        Warming Grain-free Cereals with Pears 35

****************MEDICAL MEDIUM****************

- Blackberry Power Smoothie..36
- Goji Grapefruit Parsley Smoothie 37
- Berry Clafoutis...38
- Turmeric Chai Latte (dairy free)..39
- German One Pan Pancakes Recipe (Grain Free, Gluten Free) 41
- Paleo Coconut Flour Waffles Recipe 42
- Chocolate Almond Butter Smoothie (Dairy Free) Recipe 43
- Coconut Macaroon Smoothie (Dairy Free) Recipe 44
- Acai Chocolate Smoothie (Dairy Free) 45
- Triple Berry Smoothie (Dairy Free) Recipe 46
- Sweet Potato Smoothie (Dairy Free) Recipe 47
- Primal Porridge 48
- Raw Chia Spice Pudding Recipe 49
- Black Bean Open Faced Omelet Recipe 50
- Mushroom Cheddar Omelet Recipe 51
- Primal Hemp Cereal with Coconut & Blueberries Recipe 52
- Spinach, Tomato & Feta Scramble Recipe 53
- Ultra Greens Elixir Recipe...54
- Huevos Rancheros Recipe 55
- Primal Breakfast Tostado Recipe 56
- Primal Nutmeal with Raspberries & Pumpkin Seeds Recipe 58
- Coconut Waffles...59
- Coconut Pancakes Recipe 60
- Breakfast Quinoa with Blueberries Recipe 61
- Organic Cottage Cheese with Ripe Strawberries & Sliced Almonds Recipe 62
- Avocado, Coconut & Sliced Almond Salad with Honey Drizzle Recipe 63
- Coconut Breakfast Quinoa Recipe 64
- Chocolate, Peanut Butter & Banana Smoothie (Vegan) Recipe 65
- Greek Yogurt & Berries Recipe..66

Avocado, Coconut & Sliced Almond Salad with Honey Drizzle Recipe 67

Sweet Potato Smoothie Recipe 68

Southwestern Scramble Recipe 69

Crustless Crab Quiche Recipe 70

Greek Frittata with Spinach, Feta & Olives Recipe 71

Asparagus & Sun-Dried Tomato Frittata Recipe 72

Blueberries & Cottage Cheese Recipe 73

Triple Berry Smoothie Recipe 74

Thyroid Healing Delectable Dessert Recipes 75

Creamy Lime Pudding 75

Ginger and Mint Strawberry Cobbler 76

Chocolate Addiction Smoothie with Avocado and Cacao Powder 78

Poppy Seed-Stuffed Apples 79

Gluten Free Ice Cream Sandwiches (Dairy Free, Low Sugar) 80

Dairy Free Pumpkin Souffles Recipe 82

Gingerbread Cookies (Gluten Free, Dairy Free, Vegan) Recipe 84

German Chocolate Cake Frosting (Sugar Free, Dairy Free) Recipe 86

Coconut Creme Brulee (Dairy Free) Recipe 87

Carrot Cake Cupcakes (Gluten Free, Dairy Free, Sugar Free) Recipe 89

Apple Streusel (Low Carb, Gluten Free) Recipe 90

Banana Walnut Muffins (Sugar Free, Gluten Free, Dairy Free) Recipe 92

Blueberry Pie (Low Carb, Gluten Free, Dairy Free) Recipe 94

Coconut Cupcakes (Grain Free, Gluten Free, Low Carb) Recipe 96

Yellow Cupcakes (Gluten Free, Dairy Free) Recipe 98

Almond Joy Chocolate Bark Recipe 100

Apple Streusel Recipe 101

Black Bean Brownies Recipe 102

Raw Chocolate Avocado Mousse Recipe 103

Fresh Berries & Cashew Vanilla Cream Recipe 104

############***MEDICAL MEDIUM***############

Raspberry Custards Recipe 105

Coconut Ice Cream (Dairy Free, Sugar Free) Recipe 106

Cranberry Pecan Bread Recipe 107

Coconut Cheesecake Squares Recipe 109

Flourless Peanut Butter Cookies Recipe 110

Chocolate Rum Balls Recipe 111

Thyroid Healing Delectable Salad recipe 112

Arugula Chicken Salad with Olives & Pecans Recipe 112

Simple Greek Salad Recipe 114

Arugula Salad with Salmon, Tomato and Avocado Recipe 116

Poached Salmon Spinach Salad Recipe 117

Cucumber, Red Onion & Feta Salad with Mint Recipe 119

Romaine Salad with Red Onions, Cucumber and Feta Cheese Recipe 120

Asparagus Sesame Salad Recipe 121

Pecan Chicken Salad with Green Apple Vinaigrette Recipe 122

Lemon Chicken Salad with Tarragon Recipe 123

Arugula Salad with Chicken and Avocado Recipe 124

Spinach, Apple, and Walnut Salad Recipe 125

Minted Cucumber Salad with Indian-Spiced Dressing Recipe 126

Crab & Avocado Salad Recipe 127

Mexican Salad with Black Beans & Avocado-Cilantro Dressing Recipe 128

Dill Salmon Salad Over Spring Mix Recipe 129

Shrimp Caesar Salad Recipe 130

Arugula, Fig & Gorgonzola Salad Recipe 132

Baby Spinach Salad with Creamy Italian Dressing Recipe 133

Thyroid Healing Delectable Salad dressing 134

Paleo Macadamia Mayonnaise Recipe 134

Cherry Balsamic Vinaigrette Recipe 135

Buttermilk Ranch Dressing Recipe 136

Tomato Mayonnaise (Vinegar Free) Recipe 137
Basic Vinegar-Free Salad Dressing Recipe 138
CONCLUSION: 139

Introductions:
It Time for You to Take Control and Become a True Thyroid Expert

Hashimoto's thyroiditis is not only the most common form of thyroiditis (thyroiditis), but also the most common thyroid disorder in the United States. Disease, also known as chronic lymphocytic thyroiditis or autoimmune thyroiditis, affects only 14 million people in the United States.

Hashimoto's thyroiditis was named after a Japanese physician who discovered it in 1912. It is an autoimmune disease, meaning it occurs when immune cells attack healthy tissue instead of protecting it. In Hashimoto's thyroiditis, immune cells erroneously attack healthy thyroid tissue, cause inflammation thyroid. Autoimmune diseases affect women more than men, and women are 7 times more likely to have Hashimoto's thyroiditis.

When your thyroid gland is attacked by immune cell dysfunction, which affects the thyroid's ability to produce thyroid hormones. This can lead to hypothyroidism. Hashimoto's thyroiditis is the most common cause of hypothyroidism.

If Hashimoto's thyroiditis attacks your thyroid gland to such an extent that it cannot produce enough thyroid hormones for your body to function properly, it will develop hypothyroidism. But hypothyroidism is not the only complication associated with Hashimoto's thyroiditis. In some people, the disorder causes inflammation and hypertrophy of the developing thyroid.

Hashimoto's disease affects thyroid function. Also called chronic lymphocytic thyroiditis or just chronic thyroiditis. In the United

States Hashimoto is the most common cause of hypothyroidism (sub-thyroid).
Your thyroid press releases hormones that regulate metabolism, body temperature, muscle strength and many other body functions.

Causes of Hashimoto's Disease?

Hashimoto's disease is an autoimmune disease. The condition is created by antibodies that attack the thyroid cells. Physicians do not know why this is happening, but some scientists believe that genetic factors can be major cause.

The cause of Hashimoto's disease remains unknown. However, several risk factors for this disease have been identified. Seven times it is more likely to occur in women than in men, especially in women who are pregnant. Your risk may also be higher if you have a family history of autoimmune diseases including: Graves' disease, Type 1 diabetes, lupus, rheumatoid arthritis, vitiligo and Addison's disease.

Symptoms of the Hashimoto's disease?

The symptoms of Hashimoto's are not unique to the disease. Instead, it causes the symptoms of the sub-thyroid. Signs that your thyroid gland do not work properly include: dry, pale skin, high cholesterol, lower body muscle weakness, irregular or heavy periods, feeling sluggish, constipation, hoarse voice, depression, fatigue, cold intolerance thinning hair, problems with fertility.

However, you can have Hashimoto many years before you feel the symptoms. Disease can progress for a long time before it causes significant damage to the thyroid gland. Some people with this condition develop an increased thyroid gland. Known as drowsiness, this can cause swell in front of your neck. Guevara rarely causes pain. It may be difficult to swallow or feel full throat.

Your doctor may suspect this condition if you have insufficient thyroid symptoms. If so, check your thyroid hormone (TSH) level with your blood test. This joint test is one of the best ways to detect Hashimoto. TSH levels are high when thyroid activity is low because the body is trying to strongly stimulate the thyroid to produce more thyroid hormones. Doctors also use blood tests to check your levels of other thyroid hormones, antibodies and cholesterol.

Treatment of Hashimoto's Disease

Not everyone with Hashimoto needs treatment. If your thyroid works normally, your doctor may just want to keep track of your changes.

If your thyroid gland does not produce enough hormones, you may need medication. Levothyroxine is a synthetic hormone that replaces the unavailable thyroid hormone thyroxine. There are no side effects. If you need this medicine, you will probably be an addict for the rest of your life.

Regular use of levothyroxine may reduce thyroid hormone levels to normal. When this happens, the symptoms usually go away. However, you may need periodic testing to monitor your hormone levels. This allows your physician to adjust the dose as needed.

Some supplements and medications may affect the ability of your body to absorb levothyroxine. It is important you bring to the notice of your doctor about other medications you are taking. Some products known to cause levothyroxine problems include: Proton pump inhibitors, iron additives, acid reflux treatment, calcium supplements, Some medications for cholesterol and estrogen

You may need to adjust the time you take your thyroid medicines when you take other medicines. Some foods may also affect the absorption of this drug. Talk to your doctor about the best way to take thyroid medicines that fit your diet.

Complications related to Hashimoto

If not treated, Hashimoto's disease can cause complications, some of which may be serious. This may include: anemia, high cholesterol, Heart problems, Confusion and loss of consciousness, Reduced libido and depression. Hashimoto can also cause complication during pregnancy. Recent studies have shown that women with this condition are more likely to develop babies with cardiac, cerebral and renal abnormalities.

To limit these complications, it is important to monitor thyroid function during pregnancy in women with thyroid problems.

****************MEDICAL MEDIUM****************

Diet Recipes to Help You Take Control of your Health and Become a True Thyroid Expert

Thyroid Healing Delectable Breakfast Recipes

Farmer's Wife Sunday Breakfast

Serves: 6

Ingredients

Sausage

    1 lb. of ground lamb

    2 teaspoons of ground fennel seed

    2 tablespoons of coconut aminos

    1 tablespoon of ghee

    1 teaspoon of sea salt

    2 tablespoons of apple cider vinegar

Plate (for 1)

    A handful of organic green mix (e.g. mizuna, arugula, baby kale, etc.)

    1 tablespoon of olive oil

    pinch of salt

    ½ avocado

    1 cup of ferments (cauliflower and sauerkraut)

    juice from (½) lemon

Directions:

1. First, you mix all remaining sausage ingredients (except for the ghee) kneading well (**NOTE:** taste and adjust flavors as you like).
2. After which you shape your sausage to your desired form (maybe round or long).
3. After that, you heat up a skillet with ghee in it.
4. At this point, you add sausages and fry them for approx. 7 minutes on one side and 4 minutes on the other.
5. Then you mix green salad mix with olive, lemon and salt and toss until all the baby leaves are well covered.
6. Finally, you place greens on a large plate, then add your sausage, avocado and ferments to the plate.

Balancing Pumpkin Smoothie

Serves: 1-2

Ingredients

- ½ cup of pumpkin puree (from BPA-free can or, steamed and scooped out fresh pumpkin)
- 2 tablespoons of flax seed
- ¼ inch of fresh ginger root (grated)
- 1 tablespoon of coconut butter
- ¼ teaspoon of pure vanilla extract
- pitch of sea salt
- 1½ cups of lukewarm water
- ¼ cup of pecans
- A handful of dandelion leaves
- 1 tablespoon of tahini
- One date (pitted)
- ¼ teaspoon of cinnamon
- ¼ teaspoon of camu camu

Directions:

1. First, you put all the ingredients in the blender and puree until silky smooth.

Warming Amaranth Porridge

Serves: 2

Ingredients

- 4 cups of filtered water
- ½ teaspoon of cumin
- ½ inch fresh ginger (julienned)
- ½ teaspoon of apple cider vinegar (ACV) or lemon
- handful of raw pumpkin seeds
- 1 cup of amaranth
- 1 tablespoon of ghee
- ½ teaspoon of mustard seeds
- ½ teaspoon of sea salt
- 1 teaspoon of dry turmeric
- 1 tablespoon of raw unsalted butter or ghee

Directions:

1. First, you use a heavy-bottom pan to melt the ghee and add ginger, cumin and mustard seeds when hot.
2. After which, when mustard seeds start popping, add water, amaranth and salt.
3. After that, you bring to boil, then put on low-medium fire and cook covered for 25-30 minutes or until creamy and thick.

4. Then you take off the stove and add butter (or ghee), ACV and turmeric.
5. Finally, you sprinkle with pumpkin seeds.

Note:

1. You can replace amaranth with almond flour, ghee with coconut oil (if sensitive to dairy), amaranth with plantain flour and pumpkin seeds with 2 tablespoons of shredded coconut.
2. Feel free to skip the cumin and mustard seeds.

Oyster Pancake as Thyroid Diet Foods

Serves: 4

Ingredients

- 8oz. of fresh oysters (NOTE: you can also substitute with smoked ones from a can)
- 1 large leek (sliced in rings)
- 1 handful of parsley (chopped)
- 2 tablespoons of fish sauce
- 1 cup of rice flour
- 2 tablespoons of lard, beef tallow, ghee or better still coconut oil
- 6 small eggs (or better still 4 large ones)
- 1 red (or better still green pepper)
- 1 stick celery (chopped)
- 1 sprig of fresh rosemary (finely chopped)
- 1 teaspoon of sea salt
- 1 teaspoon of baking powder (you can skip it if you are following the Thyroid-GAPS diet)

Directions:

1. First, you roast the pepper directly over stove fire (you need not worry the skin will burn but the pepper will be intact) making sure you turn it every few minutes till it's well charred and the skin peels off easily.

2. After which you melt the fat in a large frying pan and Sautee the leeks and celery till soft and slightly browned.
3. After that, you add roasted pepper, chopped to smaller pieces.
4. Then you beat the eggs in a separate bowl, then add oysters, salt, fish sauce, parsley and rosemary.
5. At this point, you combine the dry ingredients: rice flour and baking powder in another bowl.
6. This is when you slowly stir in the dry ingredients to the egg bowl to make a smooth batter.
7. Furthermore, you add the batter to the Sautee veggies, give them a gentle stir and cover.
8. Finally, you cook on reduced fire for about 15-20 minutes till the top is firm.

Tip: If you want you turn the pancake over to another frying pan (same size) to let the top cook even more.

Egg-free Gluten-free Pancake

Serves: 2

Ingredients

    1 cup of water

    1 tablespoon of coconut oil or better still ghee

    1 cup of garbanzo flour (**NOTE:** if you want a softer pancake, like a French crepe, I suggest you use only ⅔ of a cup)

    Pinch of salt

Directions:

1. First, you mix garbanzo flour and salt with water to a smooth paste.
2. After which you melt coconut oil or ghee in a stainless steel or cast iron pan.
3. After that, you pour the batter to the pan and tilt it so the batter fills up all sides of the pan.
4. Then you cover, lower flame to low/medium and cook for about 5-7 minutes.

NOTE: If you want your pancake soft, this is sufficient but if you like them harder and dry, flip the pancake.

I suggest you serve with any filling ideas of your choice: smoked fish + dill, apple or cherry butter, sautéed veggies + salsa, avocados + sardines, mashed sardines + cherry jam, sauerkraut+ hot sauce, coconut butter and sausage.

Paleo Wild Blueberry Bagels

Makes about 4 bagels

Ingredients

Dry Ingredients:

½ teaspoon of xanthan gum

½ cup of coconut flour

1 teaspoon of baking powder

3 tablespoons of ground flax

2 teaspoons of cinnamon

½ cup of potato starch

1 teaspoon of baking soda

Wet Ingredients:

½ cup of apple sauce

¼ cup of cashew milk

¾ cup of frozen Wild Blueberries (thawed)

2 tablespoons of water

1 tablespoon of apple cider vinegar

Directions:

1. First, you set the oven to 350F.

2. After which you add the dry ingredients to a mixing bowl and whisk to combine.
3. After you add in a separate bowl the wet ingredients and mix.
4. After that, you add the dry ingredients to the wet and combine.
5. Then you form the dough into a ball with your hands.
6. At this point, you put some oil on your hands so the dough doesn't stick to them.
7. Furthermore, you break the ball of dough into 4 pieces, roughly the same size.
8. After that, you roll each ball in your hands, then push your thumb through the middle, and shape the dough into a ring around your thumb.
9. This is when you smooth the bagels as best as you can with your fingers, then lay them on a parchment paper lined baking sheet.
10. Finally, you leave a few inches between each bagel on the sheet and then you bake the bagels for about 25 minutes.

Baked Stuffed Pumpkin

Serves: 6-8

Ingredients

2 cups of brown rice (cooked)

1½ cups of cranberries

2 teaspoons of salt

2 tablespoons of olive oil

1 medium size pumpkin

1 cup pecans (chopped)

1 cup of chicken stock

2 tablespoons of flax seed meal (ground flax seed)

2 stalks of sage (chopped)

Directions:

1. Meanwhile, you heat the oven to 400F (200C).
2. After which you cut the top of the pumpkin off with a sharp knife, scoop out the seeds, rub outside of the pumpkin with some olive oil.
3. After that, you make the stuffing by combining all the ingredients in a bowl.
4. Then you stuff the pumpkin and cover it with the pumpkin top.
5. At this point, you place the pumpkin on a tray and bake for an hour or until very soft when poked with a fork.
6. It can be served as a main or as a side dish.

Braised Green Cabbage

Serves: 4

Ingredients

- 1 large yellow onion (cut to thin wedges)
- ¼ cup of chicken stock or better still water
- sea salt
- 1 medium head of cabbage (cut into wedges)
- 1 large carrot (chopped to round pieces)
- ¼ cup of olive oil
- ⅛ chili flakes

Directions:

1. First, you heat the oven to 325F or 165C.
2. After which you arrange the cabbage wedges in a baking pan and scatter onion and carrot on top.
3. After that, you pour the stock into the baking pan.
4. Then you sprinkle with salt, pepper, olive oil, and chili flakes.
5. Furthermore, you cover and bake for about 1 ½ hours or till the cabbage is very tender.
6. Then you take off the cover and bake for another 15 minutes for the cabbage to get crispy and brown.

Steamed Collard Greens

Serves: 2-3

Ingredients

⅛ cup of olive oil

1 tablespoon of sesame seeds

Seaweed, like wakame (it is optional)

1 bunch of collard greens

Juice of 1 lemon

salt and pepper

Directions:

1. First, you wash and cut the collard greens into 1 ½-inch ribbons (cut out the stem).
2. After which you place in a steam basket and steam for no more than 5 mins.
3. If you using wakame seaweed, I suggest you soak for 5-10 mins (please follow instructions).
4. After that, you combine lemon juice, olive oil, salt and pepper into a dressing.
5. Then you toast sesame seeds on a pan, being careful not to burn them.
6. Finally, you pour dressing over collard greens and add the sesame seeds and seaweed.

Roasted Brussel Sprouts and Grapes

Serves: 8 servings

Ingredients

- 1 pound of red seedless grapes
- 2 cloves garlic (sliced)
- salt and black pepper
- 1½ pounds of brussels sprouts (trimmed and halved)
- 3 tablespoons of olive oil
- 1 teaspoon of fresh thyme leaves
- 3 sprigs of tarragon leave (chopped)

Directions:

1. First, you heat the oven to 375° F (or 190 C).
2. After which you toss the Brussels sprouts and grapes with the garlic, tarragon, oil, thyme, ½ teaspoon salt, and ¼ teaspoon pepper on a large rimmed baking sheet.
3. After that, you turn the Brussels sprouts cut-side down and roast for about 40 minutes until golden brown and tender.
4. Then you serve over brown rice or quinoa.

Salmon Goes Dancing with Salsa Verde

Serves: 4 servings

Ingredients

>Tomatillo Salsa Verde

>4 salmon fillets (pick wild Alaskan salmon)

>1 tablespoon of butter, from grass-fed or better still pasture-fed cow milk

Directions:

1. First, you spread the butter around the baking dish.
2. After which you place the salmon in the baking dish.
3. After that, you heat grill to medium-high (about 350F (175C).
4. Then you bake the salmon, skin side down for about 9-12 minutes until golden brown.
5. Furthermore, you make sure you do not overcook it as then the salmon turns dry and hard.
6. Finally, you place the salsa Verde on top of each salmon steak.

Easy Thai Salmon

Serves: 4-6

Ingredients

    Grated rind of one lime

    3 tablespoons of coconut aminos (NOTE: this is to replace soy sauce)

    2 tablespoons of fish sauce

    1 tablespoon of freshly grated ginger

    3 garlic cloves (minced)

    2 pounds of wild salmon filets

    4 tablespoons of sesame seeds

    2 tablespoons of lime juice

    2 tablespoons of toasted sesame oil

    ½ medium red onion (sliced thinly in half rings)

Directions:

1. Meanwhile, you heat oven to 350F.
2. After which you place salmon (skin down) in an oiled glass baking form.
3. After that, you zest the lime to a mixing bowl and add all the other ingredients.
4. Then you pour them over the salmon.
5. At this point, you cover with aluminum foil but don't let it touch the salmon.

6. Furthermore, you bake till salmon is just cooked (or it will get dry and hard), for about 16 minutes.
7. Finally, you slice the salmon into individual portions and serve over buckwheat or brown rice.

Wild Blueberry Apple Spiced Slow Cooker Oats

Ingredients

4 cup of unsweetened soy milk

2 cup frozen Wild Blueberries

1 Tablespoon of vanilla extract

¼ teaspoon of salt

1 cup of steel cut oatmeal

2 medium apples (diced)

2 Tablespoons of chia seeds (or better still ground flax seeds)

1 Tablespoon of Cinnamon

½ Tablespoon of ginger

Optional: walnuts, Pumpkin seeds or almond butter

Directions:

1. First, you add all ingredients to a glass mixing bowl that will fit in your slow cooker.
2. After which you fill water in the slow-cooker basin (1/-1 inch) below the top of the bowl.
3. After that, you set on low for 8 hours.
4. Then you serve plain or better still with nuts, pumpkin seeds, or nut butter.

Wild Blueberry, Cranberry and Almond Oatmeal

Serves 4

Ingredients

1 cup of vanilla-flavored almond milk

1 cup of quick-cooking steel-cut oats

Maple syrup or better still agave nectar (for serving, it optional)

2 cups of frozen Wild Blueberries

1 cup of water

¼ cup of slivered almonds

¼ cup of dried cranberries (chopped)

Directions:

1. First, you bring the almond milk and water to a boil in a medium saucepan.
2. After which you add the oatmeal and reduce the heat to low, cover, and simmer for 10 minutes until most of the liquid has been absorbed.
3. After that, you slide the pan off the heat, and let it set, still covered, for 5 minutes. (NOTE: If your oatmeal seems dry or too thick after it has rested, I suggest you stir in more almond milk until you get the desired consistency.)
4. Then you gently stir in the blueberries.
5. Finally, you top each bowl with one tablespoon almonds, one tablespoon dried cranberries, and a drizzle of maple syrup (if you using).

Dried Wild Blueberry and Almond Granola

Yields 6 lbs.

Ingredients

1 lb. of dried Wild Blueberries

8 oz. of whole wheat flour

10 oz. of coconut (unsweetened)

½ oz. of flax seeds

15 oz. of honey

11 oz. of almonds (roughly chopped)

26 oz. of rolled oats

10 oz. of brown sugar

¾ oz. of sesame seeds

11 oz. of olive oil

Directions:

1. First, you reserve the dried fruit and mix all dry ingredients together.
2. After which you add the oil and honey, mix thoroughly.
3. After that, you place the mixture on sheet pans and cook at 250°F for 1½ to 2 hours.
4. Then you stir the mixture every 15 minutes to ensure an even caramelization.
5. At this point, you add in the dried blueberries and cook for another 15 minutes.
6. Finally, you cool and serve room temperature.

Wild Blueberry Protein Smoothie

Ingredients

1 banana (frozen)

1 scoop of vanilla protein powder

1 teaspoon of vanilla extract

2-4 oz. of unsweetened coconut milk beverage (or better still your favorite milk)

1 cup of frozen Wild Blueberries

½ cup of vanilla Greek yogurt

½ teaspoon of cinnamon

1 Tablespoon of blueberry flavored ground flaxseed (in a situation where you can't find it, I suggest you use plain)

Directions:

1. First, you blend all ingredients in a high powered blender.

Coconut Peanut Butter Wild Blueberry Toast

Ingredients

1 Tablespoon of unsweetened shredded coconut

1/8 teaspoon of vanilla extract

4 slices of your favorite bread (should be cut into heart shapes and toasted)

2 heaping Tablespoons of natural-style creamy nut butter (I prefer peanut butter)

1 ½ teaspoon of honey

1 cup of frozen fresh Wild Blueberries

1 teaspoon of coconut oil (melted)

Directions:

1. First, you combine nut butter, honey, frozen Wild Blueberries, vanilla and coconut in a food processor.
2. After which you process until well blended and creamy.
3. After that, you use a heart-shape cookie cutter, create 4 hearts from your bread.
4. Then you toast the heart pieces and slather with the nut Butter-Wild Blueberry mixture.
5. Finally, you top with more Wild Blueberries before serving.

Paleo, raw, gluten free, dairy free

Ingredients

- 4 cups of filter water
- ¼ teaspoon of Himalayan pink salt
- 1 cup of brazil nuts
- 1 teaspoon of vanilla extract (scrape of the vanilla pod)
- 2 medjool of dates

Directions:

1. First, you add the entire ingredients (excluding the pink salt and vanilla) to a high speed blender and whiz for a minute or until a smooth consistency is present.
2. After which you prepare a large jug with a cheesecloth over the top and begin to pour the nut milk into the cheesecloth.
3. After that, you squeeze the excess bits of milk out of the pulp that is compressed into the cheesecloth.
4. Then you add the pulp to your smoothies, as not to waste anything.
5. Finally, you remove the cheesecloth and then stir in the vanilla along with the pink salt.

Warming Grain-free Cereals with Pears

Serves: 2 servings

Ingredients

    2 tablespoons of flax seed

    2 tablespoons of pumpkin seeds

    1 pear (sliced)

    ¼ spoon of sea salt

    Hot water

    2 tablespoons of chia seeds

    2 tablespoons of hemp seeds

    ½ pod vanilla bean (spiced and seeds scooped out or better still vanilla extract)

    2 tablespoons of coconut nectar

    2 tablespoons of coconut milk

    2 tablespoons of coconut butter (it is optional)

Directions:

1. First, you grind all seeds.
2. After which you add vanilla beans or extract and sea salt.
3. After that, you pour hot water over the seeds, add coconut butter (it is optional) and cover for 10 minutes.
4. Finally, when thickened add pear slices and drizzle with coconut milk.

Blackberry Power Smoothie

Serves: 1

Ingredients

- Handful of hemp seeds
- 1 tablespoon of milk thistle
- Handful of almonds (pecans or better still walnuts)
- 1 tablespoon of coconut oil or better still ghee
- 1 teaspoon of raw honey (it is optional)
- A Handful of organic blackberries
- 1 ½ tablespoons of ground flax seed (a.k.a flax seed meal)
- ½ teaspoon of camu camu powder
- 1 cup of warm water
- 1 tablespoon of pumpkin seeds (it is optional)

Directions:

1. First, you combine all ingredients in a blender.
2. Then you blend till it's either very smooth or somewhat smooth if you like chunks in your smoothie.

Goji Grapefruit Parsley Smoothie

Serves: 1

Ingredients

> ½ grapefruit
>
> A Handful of hemp seeds
>
> 1 tablespoon of milk thistle
>
> 1 cup of filtered water
>
> A Handful of dry goji berries that have been soaked
>
> A Handful of fresh parsley
>
> 1 ½ tablespoons of ground flax seed (also known as flax seed meal)
>
> A Handful of almonds (pecans or better still walnut)

Directions:

1. First, you soak the goji berries for or at least two hours or overnight.
2. After which you combine all ingredients in a blender.
3. Then you blend until it either very smooth or somewhat smooth if you like chunks in your smoothie.

Berry Clafoutis
Serves: 12

Ingredients

1 tablespoon of organic coconut oil

1 cup of coconut milk

3 tablespoons of coconut flour

½ teaspoon of sea salt

2 cups of fresh or frozen berries (I prefer to use blackberries and raspberries)

2 eggs

⅓ cup of coconut nectar (or better still any sugar you like)

½ teaspoon of vanilla extract

Directions:

1. Meanwhile, you heat the oven to 400F (or 200C).
2. After which you spread some coconut oil at the base of a 9-inch pie dish.
3. After that, you put the berries in the baking dish and put them in the oven for 5-10 minutes for them to start "sweating."
4. Then you combine all the remaining ingredients (NOTE: I will suggest that you mix dry ingredients and wet ingredients separately, combine them then by whisking them into a smooth batter).
5. At this point, you take out the dish from the oven and pour the batter over the fruit.
6. Finally, you bake for 20-25 minutes, or until the middle is firm.

Turmeric Chai Latte (dairy free)

Serves: 2

Ingredients

Masala chai mix

1 large Ceylon cinnamon stick (broken to pieces)

8 crushed cardamom pods

½ teaspoon of black pepper corns (crushed)

3 cups of water

2 teaspoons of rooibos (or better still black tea)

2-inch of fresh ginger root (sliced)

5 cloves (crushed)

1 teaspoon of fennel seed

Other ingredients include:

2 pitted dates

3 tablespoons ghee (or better still coconut butter)

1 teaspoon of turmeric

¼ teaspoon of vanilla powder (it is optional)

½ teaspoon of nutmeg powder (it is optional)

Directions:

1. First, you place the water and the masala chai mix in the saucepan and bring water to a boil.
2. After which you reduce the heat and simmer for about 10-15 minutes.
3. After that, you strain and transfer to the blender.
4. Then you add dates and ghee and blend on high for 1 minute.
5. Furthermore, you add turmeric powder and blend again for a few seconds.
6. Finally, you pour to serving glasses and sprinkle with vanilla powder and nutmeg powder.

German One Pan Pancakes Recipe (Grain Free, Gluten Free)

Serves: 12

Ingredients

    1 cup of almond meal

    12 large pastured eggs (beaten)

    1 teaspoon of cinnamon

    4 Tablespoons of virgin coconut oil

    ¼ teaspoon of Celtic Sea Salt

    1 cup of fresh shredded (unsweetened coconut)

Directions:

1. Meanwhile, you heat oven to 325 degrees F.
2. After which you put the coconut oil in an 11x13 baking dish and put in the oven for about 5 minutes, until melted.
3. After that, you combine the rest of the ingredients in a large mixing bowl and pour into the hot pan.
4. Then you bake for about 15-20 minutes until the center is cracked and the sides are pulling away from the pan.
5. Finally, you slice and serve warm with fresh fruit or pure maple syrup.

Paleo Coconut Flour Waffles Recipe

Serves: 4

Ingredients

- 8 drops of Sweet Leaf Stevia Clear Liquid Stevia
- 5⅓ Tablespoons of Bob's Red Mill Organic Coconut Flour
- ½ teaspoon of Celtic Sea Salt
- 6 large pastured eggs
- ½ teaspoon of non-aluminum baking powder
- 4 Tablespoons of Kerry gold Irish Butter

Directions:

1. First, you put the butter and eggs in a blender and blend until well combined.
2. After which you add the stevia, salt and baking powder, and mix to combine.
3. After that, you add coconut flour and blend until there are no lumps.
4. Then you pour the batter into a preheated, greased waffle iron and cook until waffles are golden brown.
5. It is best eaten warm.

Chocolate Almond Butter Smoothie (Dairy Free) Recipe

Serves: 1

Ingredients

      One cup of spring (or better still filtered water)

      One Tablespoon of Maranatha (No Stir Almond Butter, Creamy)

      One Scoop Jay Robb Chocolate Egg White Protein

Directions:

1. First, you add all ingredients + 2-3 ice cubes in a blender or Magic Bullet.
2. Then you blend until smooth.
3. Finally, you serve.

Coconut Macaroon Smoothie (Dairy Free) Recipe

Serves: 1

Ingredients

- 1 teaspoon of organic extra virgin coconut oil
- ½ packet of Sweet Leaf Sweetener
- One Scoop Jay Robb Vanilla Egg White Protein
- 2 Tablespoons of dried unsweetened organic coconut (shredded)
- 1 cup filtered or better still spring water

Directions:

1. First, you add all ingredients to the blender.
2. After which you add 2 ice cubes, or more as desired.
3. Then you blend until smooth, adding more water to reach desired consistency.
4. You can now serve.

Acai Chocolate Smoothie (Dairy Free)

Serves: 1

Ingredients

- One Scoop Jay Robb Chocolate Egg White Protein
- ½ packet of Sweet Leaf Sweetener
- ½ cup of spring water
- ½ Serving Sambazon Acai Smoothie Pack
- ⅓ cup of frozen wild organic blueberries

Directions:

1. First, you add all ingredients to a blender.
2. Then you blend until smooth.

Triple Berry Smoothie (Dairy Free) Recipe

Serves: 2

Ingredients

- ½ cup of organic frozen strawberries
- 2 cup of filtered or better still spring water
- 2 Scoops Jay Robb Strawberry Egg White Protein
- ⅓ cup of organic frozen blueberries
- ⅓ cup of organic frozen raspberries
- 4 drops Sweet Leaf Stevia Clear Liquid Stevia

Directions:

1. First, you add all ingredients to a high speed blender or Vitamix.
2. Then you blend until smooth.

Sweet Potato Smoothie (Dairy Free) Recipe

Ingredients

- 1 cup of spring or better still filtered water
- ½ cup of Pacific Organic Almond Milk (Plain)
- ½ packet of Sweet Leaf Stevia Plus Sweetener
- 1 medium organic sweet potato (baked, peeled, cooled)
- 2 scoops of Jay Robb's Vanilla Sprouted Brown Rice Protein Powder

Directions:

1. First, you add all ingredients to a blender or a Magic Bullet with 2-3 ice cubes.
2. After which you add more water to achieve desired consistency.
3. Then you blend until smooth.

Primal Porridge
Serves: 2

Ingredients

    ½ packet of Sweet Leaf Stevia Plus Sweetener

    2 Tablespoons of Bob's Red Mill Organic Coconut Flour

    ½ teaspoon of organic cinnamon

    2 Tablespoons of organic walnuts (chopped)

    2 large organic eggs

    2 Tablespoons of organic virgin coconut oil (melted)

    ½ cup of filtered or better still spring water

Directions:

1. First, you whisk together eggs, melted coconut oil, salt, coconut flour, stevia and water in a saucepan until smooth.
2. After which you cook over medium heat, stirring occasionally for about 5-7 minutes until water is absorbed and a porridge-like consistency is reached.
3. Then you top with nuts and cinnamon.
4. Finally, it now ready to serve.

Raw Chia Spice Pudding Recipe

Serves: 1

Ingredients

- ¾ cup of filtered or better still spring water
- 5 drops of liquid stevia extract
- ¼ teaspoon of organic nutmeg
- 1 oz. of organic raw cashews
- ¼ teaspoon of organic cinnamon
- 2 tablespoons of organic raw chia seeds

Directions:

1. First, you add all ingredients to a VitaMix or high speed blender.
2. Then you blend until smooth.
3. You can now serve.

Black Bean Open Faced Omelet Recipe

Ingredients

¼ teaspoon of Celtic sea salt

1 Tablespoon of fresh cilantro (chopped)

4 large organic eggs

½ cup of Eden Foods Refried Black Beans Eden Black Beans

2 oz. organic cheddar cheese (shredded)

¼ teaspoon of freshly ground black pepper

2 teaspoons of organic avocado oil

¼ teaspoon of organic chili powder

Directions:

1. First, you heat oil in a large, safe nonstick skillet over low heat.
2. After which, you beat the chili powder, salt, egg, egg whites and pepper together.
3. Then you increase the temperature of the skillet to medium-high and swirl to ensure oil completely coats the bottom of the pan.
4. After that, you pour in the egg mixture and swirl to evenly coat the pan.
5. At this point, you gently pull the edge of the eggs that have set away from the side of the pan with a rubber spatula, and tilt the pan allowing the uncooked egg to flood the bottom of the pan.
6. Furthermore, you continue the tilt and flood process until top of omelet is wet, but not runny.
7. After which you top the omelet with the black beans, cheese, cilantro and turn heat to low.
8. Finally, you cover and cook for about 2 minutes more to melt cheese.
9. You can now serve.

Mushroom Cheddar Omelet Recipe

Serves: 1

Ingredients

- 2 large organic (pasture-raised egg whites)
- 1 pinch of Celtic sea salt
- ¾ cup of organic crimini mushrooms
- 2 large organic pasture-raised eggs
- ¼ teaspoon of freshly ground black pepper
- 2 Tablespoons of chopped organic onion
- One oz. raw, organic cheddar cheese (grated)

Directions:

1. First, you add the eggs and egg whites to a medium bowl and then whisk well.
2. After which you heat a medium, safe, nonstick pan over medium heat.
3. After that, you spray with organic high heat cooking spray.
4. Then you add the onions and cook for about a minute; add the mushrooms and cook for 2 minutes.
5. At this point, you drain and return to heat.
6. Furthermore, you pour in the egg mixture and cook until set on the bottom.
7. After which you sprinkle with cheese and fold omelet in half.
8. Then you cook omelet just until eggs have set and cheese is melted.
9. You can now serve.

Primal Hemp Cereal with Coconut & Blueberries Recipe

Serves: 1

Ingredients

- 1 Tablespoon of organic shredded unsweetened coconut
- One serving Nutiva Organic Shelled Hemp Seed
- ½ cup of organic frozen blueberries (thawed with juice)

Directions:

1. First, you add thawed blueberries with juice to a bowl.
2. Then you mix in hemp and coconut.
3. You can now serve.

Spinach, Tomato & Feta Scramble Recipe

Serves: 2

Ingredients

- 1 medium organic tomato (diced)
- 2 cup of Earthbound Farm Baby Spinach
- 1 ½ oz. of organic feta cheese (crumbled)
- 4 large pasture-raised egg whites
- 6 large pasture-raised eggs

Directions:

1. First, you heat a medium, safe nonstick pan over medium heat.
2. After which you spray with organic, high heat spray.
3. After that, you add tomatoes and spinach.
4. Then you sauté for about 2 minutes until tender.
5. At this point, you whisk eggs and egg whites and pour over spinach and tomatoes.
6. After that, you cook, stirring, over medium-low heat until almost set.
7. Finally, you add the cheese, stir to incorporate.
8. Then you serve.

Ultra Greens Elixir Recipe

Serves: 1

Ingredients

- 1 teaspoon of Carlson Cod Liver Oil
- One serving Dr. Sears Primal Force Ultra Greens
- 2 large organics, pasture-raised eggs

Directions:

1. First, you add all ingredients to a blender of Magic Bullet.
2. Then you blend well to combine.
3. You can now serve.

Huevos Rancheros Recipe

Serves: 4

Ingredients

      1 cup of organic salsa

      8 large organic omega-3 eggs

      ½ medium organic avocado (sliced)

      1 cup of Eden Organic Refried Pinto Beans

Directions:

1. First, you heat two safe, nonstick pans over medium heat.
2. After which you coat both with nonstick spray.
3. After that, you spread beans in one pan to heat through.
4. Furthermore, in the other pan, crack the eggs and cook to desired temperature.
5. At this point, you transfer eggs and beans to serving plates.
6. Finally, you top with salsa and avocados.
7. You can now serve.

Primal Breakfast Tostado Recipe

Serves: 2

Ingredients

- 2 whole organic limes (juiced)
- ½ large organic onion (diced)
- ½ teaspoon of Celtic sea salt
- 1 clove organic garlic (minced)
- ¼ teaspoon of chili powder
- 2 medium organic tomatoes (finely diced)
- 1 teaspoon of paprika
- 1 Tablespoon of organic cilantro (chopped)
- ½ medium organic avocado
- 1 Tablespoon of organic extra virgin olive oil
- 4 large pasture-raised eggs

Directions:

1. Make the guacamole first, then you add the garlic, avocado, salt, and juice of 1 lime to a small non-reactive bowl.
2. After which you mash and set aside.
3. After that, you make the salsa.
4. At this point, you combine cilantro, chili powder, tomatoes, onions, ½ Tablespoon oil, remaining lime juice and paprika in a small non-reactive bowl. Then set aside.
5. Furthermore, you add remaining oil to a safe, nonstick pan over medium high heat.

6. After that, you beat the eggs and pour into hot pan. (NOTE: Do not touch the omelet, just swirl the pan around so that egg move around and the omelet becomes evenly cooked).
7. Then when the egg begins to slide around in the pan, flip it.
8. This is when you cook on opposite side to desired doneness.
9. Finally, you place omelet on serving plate, then you spoon guacamole mixture over the omelet and top with salsa.
10. You can now serve.

Primal Nutmeal with Raspberries & Pumpkin Seeds Recipe

Serves: 2

Ingredients

    2 Tablespoons of organic flaxseed (ground)

    ¼ oz. of raw organic pumpkin seeds

    ½ cup of organic raspberries

    ½ teaspoon of ground organic cinnamon

    ¼ teaspoon of ground organic ginger

    ½ oz. of raw organic pecans

    3 large pasture-raised eggs

    ¼ cup of Pacific Organic Almond Milk (Plain)

    1 Tablespoon of organic walnuts

    1 pinch ground organic nutmeg

Directions:

1. First, you add pecans, walnuts, flax seed and spices to a food processor or Magic Bullet.
2. After which you pulse to a coarse grain; set aside.
3. After that, you whisk together eggs and almond milk in a small saucepan until you reach a custard-like consistency.
4. Then you stir in the nut mixture; warm over medium-low heat, stirring constantly, for about 3 minutes until the mixture reaches an oatmeal-like consistency.
5. Then you top with pumpkin seeds and raspberries.
6. You can now serve.

Coconut Waffles
Serves: 8
Ingredients

½ teaspoon of aluminum free baking powder

2 large pasture-raised eggs

½ teaspoon of organic cinnamon (to taste)

1 cup of organic coconut milk

½ teaspoon of Celtic Sea Salt

½ cup of ground organic almond flour

1 cup of shredded coconut (unsweetened)

Directions:

1. First, you add eggs and coconut milk to the bowl; whisk well.
2. After which you mix in almond meal, shredded coconut, salt, baking powder and cinnamon.
3. After that, you stir to combine thoroughly.
4. Then you heat a safe waffle iron and spray with organic high heat nonstick spray.
5. At this point, you pour batter onto waffle iron and close the lid.
6. Furthermore, you cook for about 2-3 minutes.
7. Then when the waffle is done steam no longer escapes from the waffle iron and the waffle is lightly browned and crispy.
8. You can now serve.

Coconut Pancakes Recipe

Serves: 4

Ingredients

    1 pinch of organic nutmeg

    ¼ teaspoon of organic vanilla extract

    4 Tablespoons of Bob's Red Mill Organic Coconut Flour

    ¼ teaspoon of organic cinnamon

    ¼ cup of organic coconut milk

    4 large organic omega-3 eggs

Directions:

1. First, you whisk together eggs, coconut milk and vanilla in a medium bowl.
2. After which you add dry ingredients to wet and mix well to combine.
3. After that, you let batter sit for about five minutes.
4. In the meantime, you coat a safe nonstick pan with cooking spray and heat over medium heat.
5. Then you pour about ¼ cup of batter into pan for each pancake.
6. Finally, you cook until golden, then flip.
7. You can now serve.

Breakfast Quinoa with Blueberries Recipe

Serves: 4

Ingredients

- 1 cup of organic uncooked quinoa
- 1 cup of organic blueberries
- 1 packet of Sweet Leaf Sweetener
- 2 Tablespoons of organic flax seeds
- 2 cup of purified or better still spring water

Directions:

1. First, you rinse quinoa; then you add to saucepan with water.
2. After which you bring to a simmer and cook for about 15 minutes until the quinoa is tender.
3. Then you stir in the blueberries and flaxseeds.
4. Finally, you add stevia to taste.

Organic Cottage Cheese with Ripe Strawberries & Sliced Almonds Recipe

Serves: 1

Ingredients

- 1 Tablespoon of organic almonds (sliced)
- ½ cup of organic cottage cheese
- 4 medium organic strawberries (sliced)

Directions:

1. First, you add cottage cheese to a bowl.
2. Then you top with berries and almonds.
3. You can now serve.

Avocado, Coconut & Sliced Almond Salad with Honey Drizzle Recipe

Serves: 4

Ingredients

- 2 tablespoons of shredded organic coconut
- 2 teaspoons of raw honey
- 2 cup of cubes organic avocado
- 2 oz. of organic sliced almonds

Directions:

1. First, you divide avocado cubes among serving dishes.
2. After which you sprinkle with coconut and top with almond slices.
3. Then you drizzle with honey.
4. You can now serve.

Coconut Breakfast Quinoa Recipe

Serves: 4

Ingredients

- 2 cup of purified or better still spring water
- 2 Tablespoons of organic raw almonds (sliced)
- Two Servings Tropical Traditions Coconut Cream Concentrate
- 4 Tablespoons of organic shredded coconut (unsweetened)
- 1 cup of organic uncooked quinoa
- 1 teaspoon of organic cinnamon (to taste)

Directions:

1. First, you rinse quinoa; then you add to saucepan with water.
2. After which you bring to a simmer and cook about 15 minutes until the quinoa is tender.
3. After that, you stir in the cinnamon and coconut cream.
4. Then you top with coconut and almonds.
5. Finally, you add stevia to taste and serve.

Chocolate, Peanut Butter & Banana Smoothie (Vegan) Recipe

Serves: 1

Ingredients

½ Tablespoon of organic cocoa

1 scoops of Jay Robb's Chocolate Sprouted Brown Rice Protein Powder

1 cup of spring water

1 Tablespoon of organic peanut butter

½ small organic banana

Directions:

1. First, you add all ingredients to a blender with 2-3 ice cubes.
2. After which you blend until smooth.

Greek Yogurt & Berries Recipe

Serves: 2

Ingredients

> One Serving Oikos Greek Yogurt
>
> 1 cup of organic blueberries

Directions:

1. First, you place yogurt in serving dishes.
2. After which you top with blueberries.
3. You can now serve.

Avocado, Coconut & Sliced Almond Salad with Honey Drizzle Recipe

Serves: 4

Ingredients

- 2 Tablespoons of shredded organic coconut
- 2 teaspoons of raw honey
- 2 cup cubes organic avocado
- 2 oz. of organic sliced almonds

Directions:

1. First, you divide avocado cubes among serving dishes.
2. After which you sprinkle with coconut and top with almond slices.
3. Then you drizzle with honey.
4. You can now serve.

Sweet Potato Smoothie Recipe

Serves: 2

Ingredients

- 2 Servings of Jay Robb's Vanilla Whey Protein Isolate
- ½ packet Sweet Leaf Stevia Plus Sweetener
- 1 medium organic sweet potato (baked, peeled, cooled)
- 2 Tablespoons of organic heavy cream
- 1 cup of spring or better still filtered water

Directions:

1. First, you add all ingredients to a blender or with 2-3 ice cubes.
2. Then you blend until smooth.

Southwestern Scramble Recipe

Serves: 1

Ingredients

    2 Tablespoons of organic salsa

    2 large organics, omega-3 eggs

Directions:

1. First, you heat a safe nonstick pan over medium-high heat.
2. After which you whisk eggs in a small bowl.
3. After that, you pour into heated pan.
4. Then you allow to cook for about 2 minutes until eggs become opaque; add salsa.
5. Finally, you use a wooden or nonstick spatula fold eggs to cook through (**NOTE:** about 2 minutes).
6. You can now serve.

Crust less Crab Quiche Recipe

Serves: 6

Ingredients

- 2 Tablespoons of fresh organic parsley (chopped)
- 6 large organic omega-3 eggs
- 12 oz. of lump crab
- 8 oz. of organic, grass-fed Swiss cheese
- ¼ c. of organic roasted red peppers (chopped)
- ⅓ cup of chopped organic onion
- 12 oz. of organic evaporated nonfat milk

Directions:

1. Meanwhile, you heat oven to 350 degrees.
2. After which you spray quiche pan with nonstick cooking spray.
3. After that, you spread the crabmeat, onion and parsley in the bottom of the quiche pan.
4. Then you sprinkle half of the Swiss cheese over the ingredients in pan.
5. Furthermore, you crack the eggs and whisk slightly in a medium mixing bowl.
6. After that, you add the evaporated milk and whisk to mix.
7. At this point, you pour the egg mixture over the crabmeat in the quiche pan.
8. Then you top with the remaining Swiss cheese; sprinkle the roasted red pepper over the top of the quiche.
9. Finally, you place in the oven and bake for about 45 to 50 minutes or until lightly brown around the edges.
10. Make sure you insert a knife in the center to ensure quiche has set.

Greek Frittata with Spinach, Feta & Olives Recipe

Serves: 4; Ingredients

- 1 whole organic shallot (chopped)
- 1 teaspoon of fresh, organic oregano
- 4 large organic omega-3 eggs
- 2 cup of organic spinach
- 2 oz. of organic feta cheese (crumbled)
- 1 teaspoon of organic extra virgin olive oil
- 4 large organic egg whites
- 8 pieces of organic sun-dried tomatoes
- 8 large organic Kalamata olives (sliced in quarters)

Directions:

1. First, you heat oven to 425°F.
2. After which you coat individual baking dishes (one per serving) with cooking spray; set aside.
3. After that, you heat oil in a large pan over medium heat.
4. Then you add shallot and cook for 2 to 3 minute until soft but not brown.
5. At this point, you add spinach and cook for about 2 to 3 more minutes.
6. After which you remove from heat.
7. Furthermore, you lightly whisk eggs and egg whites in a bowl.
8. After that, you chop oregano, mix with feta cheese and add to eggs.
9. This is when you spoon into baking dishes, top with sun-dried tomato pieces and Kalamata olives.
10. Finally, you bake for 12 to 14 minutes until firm in the center.

Asparagus & Sun-Dried Tomato Frittata Recipe

Serves: 4

Ingredients

    2 cup of organic asparagus (blanched and chopped)

    6 large organics, omega-3 eggs

    ½ medium organic onion (diced)

    1 oz. organic Parmesan cheese (grated)

    ¼ cup of organic sun-dried tomatoes (chopped)

    ¼ cup of organic, 1 milk

    1 Tablespoon of organic butter

Directions:

1. Meanwhile, you heat oven to 325 degrees F.
2. After which you beat eggs in a large bowl; add the milk and Parmesan.
3. After that, you heat the butter in a medium oven-safe sauté pan, and add the onion.
4. Then you cook until the onion is translucent and golden.
5. Furthermore, you pour in the eggs and turn the heat down to low.
6. After that, you stir the eggs to fully cover the bottom of the pan.
7. At this point, when the eggs begin to cook and take shape, you can stir in the diced sun-dried tomatoes and asparagus.
8. This is when you place the sauté pan into the oven and continue to cook for 2 more minutes until the frittata is cooked around the edges and the center has puffed up.
9. Finally, you remove from oven; invert the frittata onto a large platter and serve immediately.

Blueberries & Cottage Cheese Recipe

Serves: 1

Ingredients

    ½ teaspoon of organic cinnamon

    ½ cup of frozen organic blueberries

    ½ packet of Sweet Leaf Sweetener

    ½ cup of organic cottage cheese

Directions:

TIPS: I suggest you thaw blueberries if using frozen.

1. First, you add cottage cheese to a bowl.
2. After which you mix in cinnamon and stevia.
3. Then you top with blueberries.

Triple Berry Smoothie Recipe

Serves: 2

Ingredients

- 2 Servings So Delicious Unsweetened Coconut Milk
- ½ cup of organic frozen strawberries
- ⅓ cup of organic frozen raspberries
- 1 scoop of Jay Robb's Vanilla Whey Protein Isolate
- ⅓ cup of organic frozen blueberries

Directions:

1. First, you add whey protein, coconut milk, strawberries, blueberries, and raspberries to a blender.
2. Then you mix on high about 2 minutes until smooth.

Thyroid Healing Delectable Dessert Recipes

Creamy Lime Pudding

Equip.: blender.

Serves: 4-6

Ingredients

- 1 cup of water
- zest of one lime (it must be organic)
- 1 teaspoon of vanilla extract
- Generous pinch of salt (NOTE: this bring out the sweetness)
- 2 teaspoons of rose petals, for decoration (it is optional)
- 1 ½ (about 8 oz.) cups of organic cashews
- ¼ cup of coconut butter
- 2 teaspoons of lime juice
- ½ teaspoon of rose water
- 6 drops of stevia (it is optional),

Directions:

1. First, you combine all the ingredients in the blender.
2. After which you blend on high for about 2 minutes or until the pudding reaches a smooth and silky consistency.
3. After that, you pour into a serving bowl or separate serving bowls and place in the fridge to chill for about an hour.
4. Then you sprinkle with rose petals and serve.

Ginger and Mint Strawberry Cobbler

Serves: 4 to 6

Ingredients

Ingredients for the filling

    2 tablespoons of lime juice and zest of one lime

    1 tablespoon ginger (grated)

    A pinch of salt

    1 pound of strawberries

    1 tablespoon of mint, finely chopped, from about 20 leaves

    1 teaspoon of vanilla powder or extract

    2 teaspoons of arrowroot or better still tapioca starch

Ingredients for topping

    ½ cup of ghee or better still coconut oil (melted)

    1 tablespoons of maple syrup

    A pinch of salt

    1 cup of finely shredded coconut flakes

    ¼ cup of arrowroot or better still tapioca starch

    ½ teaspoon of vanilla powder

Directions:

1. Meanwhile, you heat the oven to 350F.

2. After which you combine all the filling ingredients and toss to evenly cover the strawberries.
3. After that, you place in the cast iron skillet or baking dish.
4. At this point, you combine the entire topping ingredients in a separate bowl and use your hands to work the ghee/coconut oil well into the paste until it turns into a crumble.
5. Furthermore, you spread the crumble evenly on top of the strawberries.
6. Then you bake for about 30 to 40 minutes or until the topping is brown.

Chocolate Addiction Smoothie with Avocado and Cacao Powder

Serves: 2

Ingredients

- 1 whole avocado
- A Handful of goji berries, it should be presoaked for about 15 min in warm water.
- A Handful of raw pecan nuts
- A Pinch of Himalayan sea salt
- Filtered water to top up the ingredients
- 1 tablespoon ghee (melted)
- ¼ cup of raw cacao powder
- 1 large tablespoon of pumpkin seeds
- A Pinch of cinnamon
- ¼ teaspoon of pure vanilla extract
- ½ teaspoon of fresh lemon juice

Directions:

Throw all the ingredients into the blender and blend until smooth

Poppy Seed-Stuffed Apples

Ingredients

- 1 cup of poppy seeds
- 1 tablespoon of vanilla extract
- ½ teaspoon of all spice
- 2 tablespoons of coconut oil
- 12 large organic apples
- ¼ cup of honey or better still coconut nectar
- 1 cup of pecans (chopped)
- 2oz (50g) of dark orange chocolate (chopped to small pieces)

Directions:

1. Meanwhile, you heat the oven to 375F (190C).
2. After which you wash and dry the apples.
3. After that, you grease a glass baking form with half of the coconut oil.
4. Then you cut out the core of the apples using a large spoon, make sure you do not cut through to the bottom.
5. At this point, you use the rest of the coconut oil to cover the outside of each apple.
6. Furthermore, you combine honey, poppy seeds, nuts, vanilla extract, all spice and chocolate in a bowl.
7. After which you stuff apples with the filling.
8. Finally, you bake until the outside of the apples is soft.
9. Make sure you serve warm (not hot) or cold.

Gluten Free Ice Cream Sandwiches (Dairy Free, Low Sugar)

Serves: 8

Ingredients

> 4 cup of Coconut Milk Vanilla Bean (So Delicious Dairy Free No Sugar Added)
>
> ⅓ cup of organic cocoa powder
>
> 1/3 teaspoon of Celtic Sea Salt
>
> 6 large pastured eggs (separated)
>
> 1 teaspoon of organic vanilla extract
>
> 12 Tablespoons of Wholesome Sweeteners Organic Zero
>
> 15 drops of stevia (to taste)

Directions:

1. Meanwhile, you heat oven to 375 degrees F.
2. After which you grease a 15 x 10-inch jelly-roll pan and line with unbleached parchment paper.
3. After that, you add egg yolks and ½ cup erythritol in a medium bowl.
4. Then you beat with an electric mixer for about 4 minutes until light yellow and frothy.
5. At this point, you add cocoa and vanilla and mix at low speed to combine.
6. Add egg whites and salt in a separate bowl, and then beat at medium speed for about 2 minutes.
7. Furthermore, you add remaining erythritol and beat at high speed until stiff peaks form.
8. After that, you fold egg whites into cocoa mixture and gently blend.

9. Pour batter evenly into pan, after which you transfer to oven and bake until cake springs back when touched - about 15 minutes.
10. Then you use a circle cookie cutter for round sandwiches or slice cake into sandwich-sized squares.
11. This is when you allow ice cream to soften slightly; then spread between cake slices.
12. Finally, you press down gently to adhere (but do not smash cake), return to freezer for 1 hour to set.

Dairy Free Pumpkin Souffles Recipe

Serves: 4

Ingredients

- 1 cup of organic canned pumpkin
- ¼ teaspoon of Sweet Leaf Stevia Extract
- ½ teaspoon of organic ground cloves
- 2 large organic omega-3 eggs
- 1 teaspoon of organic vanilla extract
- ½ cup of organic coconut milk
- 2 Tablespoons of organic erythritol
- 1 teaspoon of organic cinnamon
- ½ teaspoon of organic ground nutmeg
- 2 large organic omega-3 egg whites

Directions:

1. Meanwhile, you heat 350 degrees F.
2. After which you lightly spray 4-4 ounce ramekins with nonstick spray.
3. After that, you separate the eggs.
4. Then add the coconut milk, pumpkin and vanilla in a medium bowl and mix well to combine.
5. At this point, you mix the erythritol, cinnamon, egg yolks, stevia, cloves and nutmeg and whisk into pumpkin mixture.
6. Beat egg whites in a clean, dry mixing bowl until stiff peaks form.
7. Then you gently fold egg whites into pumpkin.
8. Furthermore, you fill each ramekin with ½ cup of the mixture.

9. After that, you place the ramekins in the oven (NOTE: you may use a water bath, if you wish).
10. Finally, you bake for 25 minutes or until a toothpick comes out clean.

Gingerbread Cookies (Gluten Free, Dairy Free, Vegan) Recipe
Serves: 12

Ingredients

- 8 Tablespoon of Wholesome Sweeteners Organic Zero
- ½ teaspoon of Sweet Leaf Stevia Extract
- 1 teaspoon of non-aluminum baking powder
- ½ cup of organic unsweetened applesauce
- 1 teaspoon of baking soda
- 1 Tablespoon of organic apple cider vinegar
- 4 Tablespoons of organic virgin coconut oil (melted)
- ½ teaspoon of Bob's Red Mill Guar Gum
- 8 Tablespoons of Bob's Red Mill Organic Coconut Flour
- 2 teaspoons of organic ground cinnamon
- 1 cup of ground organic almond flour
- ½ teaspoon of ground cloves
- 1 teaspoon of lemon zest
- 3 Tablespoons of organic flax seed meal
- ½ teaspoon of Celtic sea salt
- 1 Tablespoon of organic vanilla extract
- 2 teaspoons of organic ginger powder

Directions:

1. Meanwhile, you heat oven to 350 degrees F.
2. After which you add erythritol to a Magic Bullet or blender and pulse to a powder consistency.
3. After that, you add vinegar, stevia, powdered erythritol, coconut oil, applesauce, flax meal, vanilla, salt, lemon zest and spices in a medium bowl.
4. Then you mix with an electric mixer to combine.
5. At this point, you whisk together the coconut flour, baking powder, almond flour, and baking soda in a small bowl.
6. Add to wet ingredients and mix to combine thoroughly.
7. Furthermore, you dust work surface with coconut flour and place dough on surface and roll out to ¼ to ⅛ inch thickness.
8. After that, you cut out with cookie cutters.
9. Finally, you bake on unbleached parchment paper lined cookie sheet for 12-15 minutes depending on thickness.

German Chocolate Cake Frosting (Sugar Free, Dairy Free) Recipe

Serves: 24

Ingredients

    2 large pastured egg yolks

    ¼ teaspoon of Sweet Leaf Stevia Extract

    ½ teaspoon of organic vanilla extract

    1 cup of organic pecans (finely chopped)

    ½ cup of organic full fat coconut milk

    4 Tablespoons of Wholesome Sweeteners Organic Zero

    4 Tablespoons of organic virgin coconut oil

    2 oz. of organic coconut flakes (unsweetened)

Directions:

1. First, you combine coconut milk, coconut oil, erythritol, egg yolks, and vanilla in a large saucepan.
2. After which you cook over low heat, stirring constantly, until thick.
3. Then you remove from heat and stir in pecans and coconut.
4. Finally, you spread on cake while still warm.

Coconut Crème Brule (Dairy Free) Recipe

Ingredients

- 8 Tablespoons of Wholesome Sweeteners Organic Zero
- 3 cup of organic full fat coconut milk
- ½ teaspoon of Sweet Leaf Stevia Extract
- 1 large pastured egg
- 2 Tablespoons of Navitas Naturals Organic Palm Sugar
- 4 large pastured egg yolks
- 2 teaspoon of organic vanilla extract

Directions:

1. Meanwhile, you heat the oven to 325 degrees F.
2. After which you add the erythritol to a Magic Bullet or Food Processor and pulse to achieve a powder consistency.
3. After that, you add the coconut milk to a saucepan and scald (bring it nearly to a boil (about 185°F, 85°C)
4. Then you whisk together the powdered erythritol, stevia, egg, egg yolks, and vanilla extract.
5. At this point, you slowly add the coconut milk, whisking constantly.
6. This is when you skim off any foam with a spoon that may have formed on the surface.
7. Pour the custard into 6 ramekins and place ramekins in a baking pan and pour enough boiling water in the pan to reach halfway up the sides of the ramekins.
8. Furthermore, you bake for about 25-30 minutes until the custard sets.

NOTE: don't over bake; remember, it should be a little soft in the center.

9. After that, you cool in the refrigerator to set (at least 4 hours).
10. Finally, before you serve, sprinkle coconut palm sugar on top of each custard.
11. Then you caramelize with a kitchen blow-torch or place under the broiler for 2-3 minutes.

Carrot Cake Cupcakes (Gluten Free, Dairy Free, Sugar Free) Recipe

Serves: 10

Ingredients

½ teaspoon of Celtic sea salt

½ teaspoon of baking soda

1 ½ cup of ground organic almond flour

2 Tablespoons of organic virgin coconut oil

8 Tablespoons of Wholesome Sweeteners Organic Zero

½ teaspoon of Sweet Leaf Stevia Extract

3 teaspoon of organic cinnamon

1 ½ cups of grated organic carrots

3 large organic pastured eggs

½ cup of organic pecans (chopped)

Directions:

1. First, you combine salt, almond flour, baking soda and cinnamon in a large bowl.
2. After which you mix together oil, erythritol, eggs and stevia in a separate bowl.
3. After that, you stir carrots and pecans into wet ingredients.
4. Then you stir wet ingredients into dry and scoop a heaping ¼ cup batter into paper lined cupcake pan.
5. Furthermore, you bake at 325° for about 18 to 22 minutes.
6. Finally, you cool to room temperature and spread with healthy frosting of choice.
7. You can now serve.

****************MEDICAL MEDIUM****************

Apple Streusel (Low Carb, Gluten Free) Recipe

Serves: 10

Ingredients

    4 Tablespoons of fresh lemon juice

    2 medium organic apples

    1 Tablespoon of ground flax meal

    1 ½ teaspoon of organic cinnamon

    ½ teaspoon of organic vanilla extract

    ½ cup of organic pecans (chopped)

    6 Tablespoons of Wholesome Sweeteners Organic Zero

    1 cup of ground organic almond flour

    ½ teaspoon of Sweet Leaf Stevia Extract

    6 Tablespoons of organic grass-fed butter

    2 medium chayote squash (peeled)

    ½ teaspoon of organic nutmeg

Directions:

1. Meanwhile, you heat oven to 350 degrees F.
2. After which you slice apples and chayote's to about ¼ inch thick and place in an over-safe baking dish with a lid.
3. After that, you combine 3 Tablespoons of erythritol, lemon juice and stevia in a small bowl; pour over apples.
4. Then you cover, transfer to oven and bake for about 30 minutes.
5. At this point, you remove apple mixture from oven and stir well to coat (**NOTE:** make sure you adjust sweetness if necessary).
6. Furthermore, you increase oven to 375 degrees F; melt butter.

7. After which you combine with remaining 3 Tablespoons of erythritol and vanilla into a small mixing bowl.
8. After that, you mix in the chopped pecans, almond flour, cinnamon, flax meal, and nutmeg to make a crumbly meal.
9. Finally, you pour streusel over the apple-chayote mixture and bake uncovered for about 45 minutes.
10. You can now serve.

Banana Walnut Muffins (Sugar Free, Gluten Free, Dairy Free) Recipe

Serves: 12

Ingredients

- 6 large pastured eggs
- 1 teaspoon of organic vanilla extract
- 10 drops of Sweet Leaf Stevia Clear Liquid Stevia Sweet Leaf Stevia Clear
- ¼ teaspoon of Celtic sea salt
- ½ cup of organic walnuts
- 8 Tablespoons of Wholesome Sweeteners Organic Zero
- ½ teaspoon of non-aluminum baking powder
- 8 Tablespoons of Bob's Red Mill Organic Coconut Flour
- 2 medium organic bananas
- 4 Tablespoons of organic virgin coconut oil

Directions:

1. Meanwhile, you heat oven to 350 degrees F.
2. After which you place an unbleached parchment paper liner on baking sheet.
3. After that, you add walnuts and toast for about 4-5 minutes.
4. Cool and chop; then using a hand-held blender, cream erythritol coconut oil until fluffy.
5. At this point, you add vanilla and eggs, one at a time, beating well after each addition.
6. This is when you sift coconut flour (NOTE: The sifted amount should be ½ cup - no more no less!)
7. Furthermore, you combine sifted coconut flour with salt, baking powder and stevia; beat into batter.

8. After that, you beat in eggs, fold in walnuts.
9. Finally, you pour batter three quarters of the way up into a muffin pan lined with greased muffin papers.
10. Then bake for about 35 minutes.

Blueberry Pie (Low Carb, Gluten Free, Dairy Free) Recipe

Serves: 8

Ingredients

- ½ teaspoon of organic cinnamon
- 10 Tablespoons of organic virgin coconut oil
- 2 Tablespoons of fresh lemon juice
- 1 Tablespoon of Bob's Red Mill Arrowroot Starch
- 5/4 cup of ground organic almond flour
- 4 cup of Cascadian Farm Organic Blueberries
- 5 Tablespoons of filtered ice water
- ½ teaspoon of Sweet Leaf Stevia Extract
- ¼ teaspoon of Celtic sea salt

Directions:

1. Meanwhile, you heat oven to 450 degrees F; melt coconut oil.
2. After which you add thawed blueberries to a large bowl.
3. After that, you sprinkle with cinnamon, lemon juice, stevia and arrowroot and stir to coat.
4. Then you combine almond flour and salt in a large mixing bowl.
5. At this point, you stir in coconut oil and mix until the mixture resembles coarse crumbs.
6. Furthermore, you mix in ice water, 1 tablespoon at a time, until the dough comes together, then you chill the dough for about 15 minutes.
7. After that, you place dough on a piece of unbleached parchment paper and roll out.

8. This is when you invert a pie dish over the dough; flip the dough over and mold to shape pie pan.
9. After which you pour in blueberry mixture and transfer to oven.
10. Finally, you bake for about 15-20 minutes or until crust is golden brown.
11. Then you cool slightly and serve.

Coconut Cupcakes (Grain Free, Gluten Free, Low Carb) Recipe

Serves: 12

Ingredients

- ¼ cup of ground organic almond flour (packed)
- ½ teaspoon of Sweet Leaf Stevia Extract Sweet Leaf Stevia Extract
- 2 cup of Bob's Red Mill Unsweetened Shredded Coconut
- ¼ cup of organic coconut milk
- 3 large pastured eggs
- 1 Tablespoon of organic vanilla extract
- 2 Tablespoons of organic virgin coconut oil
- ½ teaspoon of aluminum-free baking powder
- 8 Tablespoons of Wholesome Sweeteners Organic Zero
- 1 Tablespoon of Bob's Red Mill Organic Coconut Flour Bob's Red Mill Coconut Flour
- A pinch of Celtic sea salt

Directions:

1. First, you heat oven to 325 degrees Fahrenheit.
2. After which you line a mini muffin pan with papers and spray with coconut oil spray.
3. After that, you add in a Magic Bullet or food processor the coconut and grind into a fine meal.
4. Then you add almond flour, coconut and remaining dry ingredients to a large mixing bowl.

5. Furthermore, in a small saucepan, melt coconut oil over low heat and add vanilla extract, eggs and coconut milk and beat well.
6. After that, you add dry ingredients into wet ingredients, and mix on medium speed for about 2 minutes.
7. Then you line a mini muffin pan with mini muffin papers, and spray with extra virgin olive oil spray.
8. At the point, pour batter into mini muffin cups, about ¾ full.
9. Finally, you transfer to oven and bake for about 18-20 minutes, until springy and firm to the touch.
10. Then you cool slightly and serve.

Yellow Cupcakes (Gluten Free, Dairy Free) Recipe

Serves: 12

Ingredients

- ½ teaspoon of baking soda
- 6 tablespoons of Spectrum Organic Shortening
- One large pasture raised egg yolk
- 5 Tablespoon of Bob's Red Mill Organic Coconut Flour
- 1 ½ teaspoons of baking powder
- 2 teaspoons of organic vanilla extract
- ¾ teaspoon of Sweet Leaf Stevia Extract
- 1 16-oz can of organic cannellini beans
- 12 Tablespoons of Wholesome Sweeteners Organic Zero
- 5 large pasture raised eggs
- ½ teaspoon of Celtic sea salt

Directions:

1. Meanwhile, you heat oven to 350 degrees F.
2. After which you line a muffin tin with unbleached parchment liners and spray with cooking spray.
3. After that, you drain and rinse beans.
4. Then you add beans, vanilla, eggs and salt to a food processor; puree well.
5. Furthermore, cream shortening with stevia and erythritol until fluffy; beat in bean/egg mixture.
6. After that, you add salt, coconut flour, baking soda and baking powder.

7. At this point, beat on high speed until fluffy.
8. This is when you spoon batter into lined muffin cups to ¾ full.
9. Finally, you bake for about 25 minutes or until golden and springy to the touch.
10. After which you let cool, frost and serve.

Notes

Make sure you let cupcakes stand for about 12-24 hours in an airtight glass container allow beany flavor to dissipate.

Almond Joy Chocolate Bark Recipe

Serves: 12

Ingredients

> 10 Tablespoons of Enjoy Life Foods Semi-Sweet Chocolate Chips
>
> ¼ cup of unsweetened shredded coconut
>
> ½ cup of almonds

Directions:

1. Meanwhile, you heat oven to 350 degrees F.
2. After which you place coconut on a baking sheet and toast for about 6-8 minutes.
3. After that, you melt chocolate over very low heat.
4. Then you pour melted chocolate onto an unbleached parchment lined 8x8 inch baking dish.
5. At this point, you scatter almonds and 3 tablespoons of coconut over chocolate.
6. This is when you use a rubber spatula to spread the mixture evenly back and forth to ½ inch thickness.
7. Furthermore, you sprinkle remaining tablespoon of coconut on top of mixture.
8. After that, you place bark in fridge; let set for about 2 hours.
9. Finally, you break into squares and keep refrigerated in an airtight container.

Apple Streusel Recipe

Ingredients

- 3 large organic Granny Smith apples (chopped)
- 1 ½ teaspoons of organic cinnamon
- ⅔ cup of organic walnuts (chopped)
- ½ teaspoon of organic vanilla extract
- ½ teaspoon of organic nutmeg
- 6 Tablespoons of organic grass-fed butter
- ⅓ cup of ground organic almond flour
- 4 Tablespoons of ZSweet

Directions:

1. Meanwhile, you heat oven to 350 degrees F.
2. After which you melt butter; pour 4 Tablespoons into a small mixing bowl.
3. After that, you pour the remaining 2 Tablespoons into a medium mixing bowl.
4. Then you add cinnamon, lemon juice and nutmeg to the medium mixing bowl with the 2 Tablespoons of melted butter; stir to mix.
5. At this point, add the apples and toss to coat; after which you make the streusel.
6. This is when you add the chopped walnuts, almond flour, erythritol, remaining ½ teaspoon of cinnamon and vanilla to the small mixing bowl with the 4 Tablespoons of butter.
7. Furthermore, you stir until combined and crumbly.
8. Finally, you pour streusel over the apples and bake for about 45 minutes.
9. You can now serve.

Black Bean Brownies Recipe

Serves: 12

Ingredients

- 4 teaspoons of organic espresso powder
- 24 packets of Truvia: Nature's Calorie-Free Sweetener
- ½ cup of organic cocoa powder
- 1 Tablespoon of organic, grass-fed butter (melted)
- 2 Tablespoons of organic light sour cream
- 1 teaspoon of organic vanilla extract
- 1 ½ cups of canned organic black beans (drained and rinsed)
- Two large organic, omega-3 eggs

Directions:

1. Meanwhile, you heat oven to 350 degrees F.
2. After which you spray 8x8 glass baking dish with nonstick spray.
3. After that, you combine cocoa, coffee, beans, eggs in food processor for 2 minutes.
4. Then you add remaining ingredients and process for 1 minute until smooth.
5. Furthermore, you pour into baking dish and bake for about 28-30 minutes, turning the dish halfway through. (**NOTE:** toothpick inserted will have soft batter clinging to it).
6. Finally, you let cool in baking dish on wire rack.
7. Then you cut into 12 squares.

Raw Chocolate Avocado Mousse Recipe

Serves: 4

Ingredients

      1 cup of Pacific Organic Almond Milk (Plain)

      1 ½ oz. Navitas Naturals Organic Raw Cacao Powder

      1 medium organic avocado

      1 whole, pitted organic date (soaked)

      4 Tablespoons of raw organic almond butter

Directions:

1. First, you add all ingredients to a food processor.
2. After which you blend until creamy.
3. Then you boost sweetness with raw stevia, if you wish.
4. You can now serve.

Notes

For a raw recipe, I suggest you use fresh almond milk.

Fresh Berries & Cashew Vanilla Cream Recipe

Serves: 6

Ingredients

    1 cup of raw organic cashews

    1 teaspoon of organic vanilla extract

    3 cup of fresh organic berries

    ¾ cup of purified or better still spring water

Directions:

1. First, you soak 1 cup of cashews in 2 cups of purified water in the refrigerator for about 8-12 hours.
2. After which you discard the soaking water and rinse the nuts.
3. After that, you place in a blender or Magic Bullet the nuts and enough fresh water to allow the blender to operate.
4. Then you blend, gradually adding enough water to achieve a smooth consistency. (NOTE: this will yield 1¾ cups - 2 cups cashew cream).
5. Finally, you place berries in serving dishes, top with a dollop of cashew cream and serve.

Raspberry Custards Recipe

Serves: 12

Ingredients

- 2 Tablespoons of arrowroot
- 6 cup of organic raspberries
- ¾ cup of organic erythritol
- ½ teaspoon of organic lemon zest
- 2 large organics, omega-3 eggs
- 1 ½ cups of organic, grass-fed milk (I prefer it raw)
- ½ cup of organic, grass-fed cream (I prefer it raw)
- 1 teaspoon of organic vanilla extract
- 1 Tablespoon of fresh organic lemon juice

Directions:

1. Meanwhile, you heat the oven to 450°.
2. After which you spread ½ cup of the raspberries in each of twelve 4-ounce gratin dishes.
3. After that, you arrange the gratin dishes on 2 baking sheets.
4. Then in a bowl you whisk the milk with the cream, Zsweet, vanilla, eggs, arrowroot, lemon juice and zest until smooth.
5. Furthermore, you ladle ¼ cup of the custard into each dish; bake for about 15 minutes, until the centers are set.
6. Finally, you transfer the custards to wire racks and let stand for about 30 minutes.
7. You can now serve.

Coconut Ice Cream (Dairy Free, Sugar Free) Recipe

Serves: 8

Ingredients

- 1 Tablespoon of organic vanilla extract
- ¼ teaspoon of Sweet Leaf Stevia Extract
- A pinch of Celtic sea salt
- 3 Tablespoons of organic virgin coconut oil
- 2 cup of organic coconut milk
- 8 Tablespoons of Wholesome Sweeteners Organic Zero
- A large organic pastured egg yolk

Directions:

1. First, you add the coconut milk, coconut oil, erythritol and sea salt to a saucepan over low heat.
2. After which you whisk until erythritol crystals dissolve; remove from heat and let cool.
3. After that, you add coconut mixture to a blender with vanilla, stevia, rum and egg yolk.
4. Then you blend on high until smooth.
5. Furthermore, you pour into an ice cream maker a freeze according to manufacturer's instructions.
6. In the other hand, freeze in a glass dish covered with plastic wrap overnight.

Cranberry Pecan Bread Recipe

Serves: 12

Ingredients

- ¾ cup of purified or better still spring water
- 2 ½ teaspoons of aluminum-free baking powder
- 2 cups of whole organic cranberries (fresh or frozen)
- 2 ½ cups of ground organic almond flour
- ¼ teaspoon of Sweet Leaf Stevia Extract
- ½ cup of organic, grass-fed butter (melted)
- ½ cup of organic pecans (chopped)
- 1 cup of organic erythritol
- ⅓ cup of organic powdered egg white
- ¾ teaspoon of Celtic sea salt (fine)
- 3 large organic omega-3 eggs

Directions:

1. Meanwhile, you heat oven to 350 degrees F.
2. After which you grease the bottom of a large 10-inch loaf pan.
3. After that, you roughly chop the cranberries or pulse in a food processor.
4. Then you mix the dry ingredients together (erythritol, egg white, baking powder, salt, almond meal, stevia).
5. At this point, you mix the wet ingredients together (eggs, melted butter, water).
6. Furthermore, you mix the dry ingredients into the wet.

7. After which you fold in the pecans and the cranberries.
8. Finally, you pour batter into pan and bake for about 40-50 minutes, until top is golden brown and toothpick comes out clean.

Coconut Cheesecake Squares Recipe

Serves: 12

Ingredients

- 4 large organic omega-3 eggs
- 1 stick of organic butter
- ¼ cup of organic erythritol
- 2 packets Sweet Leaf Stevia Plus Sweetener
- 1 cup of organic coconut flour
- 8 oz. organic cream cheese
- 1 teaspoon of organic extra virgin coconut oil
- 2 teaspoons of organic vanilla extract

Directions:

1. Meanwhile, you heat oven to 350 degrees F.
2. After which you lightly coat 11 x 7 square pan with oil.
3. After that, you cream butter and cream cheese on high speed until fluffy.
4. Then you add eggs one at a time; beat well.
5. At this point, you gradually beat in erythritol, after which you add coconut flour, stevia and vanilla and beat until blended.
6. Finally, you pour into pan and bake for about 30 minutes.
7. Cool and slice into squares before serving.

Flourless Peanut Butter Cookies Recipe

Serves: 12

Ingredients

16 Tablespoons of Maranatha Natural Peanut Butter - with Salt (Creamy)

1 cup of organic erythritol

1 teaspoon of organic vanilla extract

1 teaspoon of aluminum-free baking powder

1 packet of Sweet Leaf Stevia Plus Sweetener

1 large organic egg

Directions:

1. Meanwhile, you heat oven to 350 degrees F.
2. After which you mix all ingredients in a medium bowl to form a dough.
3. After that, you drop by teaspoonful on a cookie sheet, remember that cookies will flatten as they bake.
4. Then you bake for about 8 minutes; cool and store in an airtight container.

Chocolate Rum Balls Recipe

Serves: 12

Ingredients

    1 oz. of rum or better still brandy

    2 Tablespoons of organic erythritol

    2 Tablespoons of organic butter

    1 cup of ground organic almonds

    10 drop of Sweet Leaf Stevia Clear Liquid Stevia

    ½ teaspoon of organic vanilla extract

    ½ cup of organic cocoa powder

Directions:

1. First, you mix all dry ingredients together in a medium bowl.
2. After that, you mix the vanilla, rum, using a whisk or a fork, softened butter and stevia in a smaller bowl. (tips: remember that the total liquid amount of liquid should be between 2 ½ -3 tablespoons.)
3. At this point, you add the liquid slowly to the dry ingredients and mix until it all comes together.
4. After which you roll into balls and place in an airtight container.
5. Finally, you refrigerate at least 4 hours; the flavors will mellow over the next few days.

Thyroid Healing Delectable Salad recipe

Arugula Chicken Salad with Olives & Pecans Recipe

Serves: 2

Ingredients

- 1 Tablespoon of organic balsamic vinegar
- 1 -8oz. of breast pastured chicken
- ¼ teaspoon of freshly ground black pepper
- ½ ounce of pecans (chopped)
- ½ cup of shredded organic carrots
- 2 Tablespoons of organic extra virgin olive oil
- ¼ teaspoon of Celtic Sea Salt
- 8 small organic Kalamata olives (halved)
- 3 cups of organic arugula
- 1 teaspoon of mustard powder

Directions:

1. Meanwhile, you heat a cast-iron grill pan to medium high heat.
2. After which you season the chicken breasts with salt and pepper.
3. After that, you place seasoned chicken on the grill pan and cook for about 3-4 minutes.
4. Then you flip and cook until the juices run clear; set aside to cool slightly, then slice the chicken into ¼ inch thick strips.
5. At this point, you prepare the salad and salad dressing.

6. First, you whisk the balsamic vinegar with the oil (reserving 1 teaspoon for later) and mustard in a small bowl to emulsify. Season with salt and pepper.
7. After which you place the arugula in a medium bowl and drizzle with 1 teaspoon of oil.
8. After which you gently massage to coat the leaves, then sprinkle with a small amount of sea salt.
9. Furthermore, you toss in the shredded carrots and olives.
10. Finally, you top with chicken and drizzle with dressing and chopped pecans.

Simple Greek Salad Recipe

Serves: 4

Ingredients

- 1 teaspoon of organic extra virgin olive oil
- 1 ½ cup of cherry tomatoes (halved)
- 6 cup of shredded organic romaine lettuce
- 1 cup of sliced organic red onion
- 1 Tablespoon of fresh flat-leaf organic parsley (chopped)
- 2 cloves organic garlic (minced)
- 2 oz. of organic crumbled feta cheese
- 3 Tablespoons of organic lemon juice
- 1 cup of sliced organic cucumber (peeled)
- ¾ teaspoon of dried organic oregano
- 8 large organic Kalamata olives
- ¼ teaspoon of Celtic sea salt
- 4 whole pepperoncini peppers
- ¼ teaspoon of black pepper

Directions:

1. First, you place tomatoes, onion, lettuce, and cucumber in a large bowl.
2. After which you toss to combine.

3. After that, you combine parsley with lemon juice, oil, oregano, mustard powder, salt, pepper and garlic, stirring with a whisk.
4. At this point, you spoon 1 tablespoon dressing over salad; toss to combine then divide salad between plates.
5. Finally, you top each with 4 olive halves, ½ ounce cheese, and 1 pepperoncini pepper.

Arugula Salad with Salmon, Tomato and Avocado Recipe

Serves: 4

Ingredients

- 2 Tablespoons of organic extra virgin olive oil
- 1 teaspoon of honey
- 1 medium organic avocado (sliced)
- 4 medium small organic radishes (thinly sliced)
- ½ teaspoon of Celtic sea salt
- ¼ teaspoon of freshly ground black pepper
- ¼ small organic red onion (sliced thin)
- 6 cup of Earthbound Farm Baby Arugula Earthbound Farms Arugula
- 2 Tablespoons of organic balsamic vinegar
- 2 cans of Wild Planet Alaskan Sockeye Salmon
- 1 medium organic tomato (cut into chunks)

Directions:

1. First, you drain salmon and flake into chunks
2. After which you whisk together the honey, oil, salt, balsamic vinegar, and pepper in a small bowl.
3. After that, you divide the arugula among bowls and top with the onion, radishes, avocado, tomato and salmon chunks.
4. Then you drizzle with dressing.
5. You can now serve.

Poached Salmon Spinach Salad Recipe

Serves: 4

Ingredients

- 3 medium organic tomatoes (roughly chopped)
- 1 cup of organic white wine
- 8 oz. of organic fresh spinach
- 16 oz. wild salmon
- ¼ teaspoon of freshly ground black pepper
- 1 tablespoon of flat-leaf parsley (chopped)
- 2 Tablespoons of organic extra virgin olive oil
- ¼ teaspoon of Celtic sea salt
- ½ cup of chopped organic yellow onion

Directions:

Directions on how to poach the salmon:

1. First, you bring about 1 cup of white wine and ½ cup of water to a boil in a large skillet.
2. After which you reduce the heat, add the salmon, cover, and simmer for about 6-8 minutes, or until the salmon flakes easily.
3. After that, you heat half of the oil in a skillet, over medium heat.
4. Then when hot, sauté the spinach for about 1½ minutes.
5. At this point, you add the salt and pepper and divide the spinach among plates.
6. Furthermore, you heat the remaining tablespoon of oil in the skillet.
7. After which you sauté the onion and tomatoes over medium heat for about 5-6 minute until the onion is tender.

8. Finally, you arrange the salmon on the spinach and top with the tomatoes and onion.
9. Then you garnish with parsley and serve.

Cucumber, Red Onion & Feta Salad with Mint Recipe

Serves: 4

Ingredients

- 1 Tablespoon of fresh lemon juice
- 2 medium organic cucumbers (peeled and thinly sliced)
- 3 Tablespoons of organic extra virgin olive oil
- ½ small organic red onion (thinly sliced)
- 2 oz. of organic feta cheese (cubed)
- ½ teaspoon of Celtic sea salt
- 2 Tablespoons of fresh mint leaves
- ¼ teaspoon of freshly ground black pepper

Directions:

1. Using a Magic Bullet or mortar, lightly crush the cumin, coriander and mustard seeds until very coarsely ground.
2. After which you transfer to a small skillet.
3. Then you add the coconut oil and cook over moderate heat for about 3 minutes until the seeds are fragrant and toasted.
4. At this point, you pour into a large glass bowl and whisk in the lemon juice.
5. Season with salt and pepper.
6. Finally, you add the cucumbers and mint and toss to combine.
7. You can now serve.

Romaine Salad with Red Onions, Cucumber and Feta Cheese Recipe

Serves: 2

Ingredients

- ¼ teaspoon of Celtic sea salt
- ¼ teaspoon of black pepper
- 1 teaspoon of organic extra virgin olive oil
- 1 cup of sliced organic cucumber (peeled)
- ¾ teaspoon of dried organic oregano
- 3 Tablespoons of organic red wine vinegar
- 2 cloves organic garlic (minced)
- 1 cup of sliced organic red onion
- 6 cups of shredded organic romaine lettuce
- 2 oz. organic crumbled feta cheese

Directions:

1. First, you place onion, lettuce, and cucumber in a large bowl; toss to combine.
2. After which you combine with oil, salt, vinegar, oregano, pepper and garlic, in a medium bowl stirring with a whisk.
3. After that, you divide lettuce mixture between serving dishes.
4. Then you top each serving with 2 tablespoons cheese.
5. You can serve.

Asparagus Sesame Salad Recipe
Serves: 4; Ingredients

- 2 cup of Earthbound Farm Organic Spring Mix Earthbound Farm Organic Spring Mix
- ¼ cup of Eden Organic Rice Vinegar
- 3 teaspoons of organic roasted sesame oil
- 2 Tablespoons of sesame seeds
- 2 Tablespoons of organic tamari (gluten free soy sauce)
- 2 Tablespoons of chopped fresh cilantro
- 1 pound of organic asparagus
- ¼ teaspoon of Celtic sea salt

Directions:

1. At first you blanch the asparagus.
2. After which you bring a large pan of filtered water to a boil over high heat.
3. After that, you trim the ends of the asparagus and cut the stalks diagonally into 1-inch pieces.
4. Then when it starts boiling, add the asparagus and blanch for about 2 minutes or just until bright green.
5. Furthermore, you drain in a colander and rinse under cold water to "shock" (**NOTE:** this will stop the cooking).
6. After that, you combine the soy sauce, cilantro, vinegar, sesame oil, and salt in a large bowl.
7. This is when you add the asparagus and toss well to coat.
8. At this point, you divide greens among plates.
9. Finally, you spoon asparagus onto the greens and sprinkle with sesame seeds.
10. You can now serve.

Pecan Chicken Salad with Green Apple Vinaigrette Recipe

Serves: 4; Ingredients

- 2 cup of Earthbound Farm Organic Bibb Lettuce Leaves Earthbound Farm Organic Bibb Lettuce
- 4 Tablespoons of olive oil
- ½ cup of organic pecans
- 2 Tablespoons of chopped organic shallot
- 1 cup of seedless organic red grapes (halved)
- ½ teaspoon of Celtic sea salt
- 1 teaspoon of raw honey
- 1 medium organic Granny Smith apple (finely diced)
- 1 stalk organic celery (thinly sliced)
- 2 -8oz. of breasts pasture-raised chicken breast
- 2 Tablespoons of fresh lemon juice

Directions:

1. In the first place you poach the chicken.
2. After which you bring 2 inches of filtered water to a boil in a large, 2-quart heavy saucepan.
3. After that, you add chicken and poach at a bare simmer, partially covered, for about 12 to 14 minutes until just cooked through.
4. Then while chicken cooks, whisk together lemon juice, honey, and salt in a medium bowl until honey and salt have dissolved.
5. Furthermore, you whisk in shallot and oil, then mix in apple.
6. Slice chicken and divide grapes, chicken, lettuce, pecans and celery between serving plates and drizzle with vinaigrette.
7. You can now serve.

Lemon Chicken Salad with Tarragon Recipe

Serves: 4

Ingredients

- ½ teaspoon of Celtic sea salt
- 2 stalks organic celery (chopped)
- 2 -8oz. of breasts pasture-raised chicken
- 1 ½ teaspoons of organic Dijon mustard
- ½ teaspoon of freshly ground black pepper
- ½ whole organic lemon
- 1 tablespoon of fresh tarragon leaves
- 4 Tablespoons of Wilderness Family Naturals Mayonnaise Wilderness Family Naturals Coconut Mayonnaise
- 2 Tablespoons of chopped minced shallot

Directions:

1. You poach the chicken in the first place.
2. After which you bring 2 inches of filtered water to a boil in a large, 2-quart heavy saucepan.
3. After that, you add chicken and poach at a bare simmer, partially covered, for about 12 to 14 minutes until just cooked through.
4. Then you shred cooled chicken with a fork.
5. At this point, you whisk together the shallot, lemon juice plus ½ tsp zest, salt, mayonnaise, mustard, and pepper.
6. Furthermore, you stir in the chicken and celery.
7. Finally, you sprinkle with fresh tarragon leaves.
8. You can now serve.

Arugula Salad with Chicken and Avocado Recipe

Serves: 4

Ingredients

- 2 -8oz. of breasts organic chicken breasts
- 2 Tablespoons of fresh lime juice
- 1 medium organic avocado (sliced)
- ¼ teaspoon of freshly ground black pepper
- 6 cups of Earthbound Farm Baby Arugula Earthbound Farms Arugula
- 2 Tablespoons of organic extra virgin olive oil
- 1 teaspoon of honey
- 4 medium small organic radishes (thinly sliced)
- ½ teaspoon of Celtic sea salt

Directions:

1. You poach chicken at the place.
2. After which you fill a medium saucepan halfway with filtered or spring water; bring to a boil.
3. After that, you add the chicken, reduce heat to medium, and gently simmer for 12 to 14 minutes until cooked through.
4. Then you transfer the chicken to a cutting board and let rest at least 5 minutes before slicing.
5. In the meantime, whisk together the lime juice, salt, oil, honey, and pepper in a small bowl.
6. At this point, you divide the arugula among bowls and top with the chicken, avocado, and radishes.
7. Finally, you drizzle with dressing and serve.

Spinach, Apple, and Walnut Salad Recipe

Serves: 4

Ingredients

- 8 cup of Earthbound Farm Baby Spinach
- 1 medium organic apple (cored and diced)
- 4 Tablespoons of organic lemon juice
- ½ teaspoon of Celtic sea salt
- 1 tablespoon of organic apple cider vinegar
- 3 Tablespoons of organic extra virgin olive oil
- ¼ teaspoon of freshly ground black pepper
- 1 Tablespoon of raw honey

Directions:

1. First, you add apples and half of the lemon juice in a large bowl.
2. After which you toss to coat.
3. After that, you add in spinach and walnuts.
4. Then you whisk together remaining olive oil, honey, salt, lemon juice, vinegar, and pepper to taste.
5. Finally, you pour dressing over spinach-apple mixture and serve.

Minted Cucumber Salad with Indian-Spiced Dressing Recipe

Serves: 4

Ingredients

- 3 Tablespoons of organic extra virgin olive oil
- ½ teaspoon of cumin seeds
- 1 Tablespoon of fresh lemon juice
- 2 Tablespoons of fresh mint leaves
- ¼ teaspoon of coriander seeds
- ¼ teaspoon of freshly ground black pepper
- ¼ teaspoon of mustard seeds
- ½ teaspoon of Celtic sea salt
- 2 medium organic cucumbers (peeled and thinly sliced)

Directions:

1. First you crush lightly the cumin, coriander and mustard seeds using a Magic Bullet or mortar until very coarsely ground.
2. After which you transfer to a small skillet.
3. After that, you add the coconut oil and cook over moderate heat for about 3 minutes until the seeds are fragrant and toasted. Pour into a large glass bowl.
4. Then you whisk in the lemon juice and season with salt and pepper.
5. Finally, you add the cucumbers and mint and toss to combine.
6. You can serve.

Crab & Avocado Salad Recipe

Serves: 4

Ingredients

    1 medium organic avocado (cubed)

    1 teaspoon of cumin powder

    ¼ teaspoon of Celtic sea salt

    2 bunches of organic watercress (washed, stems removed)

    2 stalks organic celery (thinly sliced)

    ½ teaspoon of paprika

    2 Tablespoons of organic lime juice

    16 oz. of sustainable lump crab meat (cooked)

    ¼ teaspoon of freshly ground black pepper

    3 Tablespoons of organic mayonnaise

Directions:

1. First, you mix lime juice, cumin, mayonnaise, and paprika in a large bowl.
2. After which you add crab meat, and celery.
3. Mix well and season with salt and pepper.
4. After that, you gently stir in avocado cubes and divide watercress on four plates.
5. Finally, you top with salad and serve.

Mexican Salad with Black Beans & Avocado-Cilantro Dressing Recipe

Serves: 4

Ingredients

- ½ can Eden Foods Organic Black Beans
- 2 Tablespoons of organic lemon juice
- ¼ teaspoon of Celtic sea salt
- ½ medium organic red onion (chopped)
- 2 Tablespoons of fresh cilantro (chopped)
- 2 heads of organic romaine lettuce (chopped)
- ½ medium organic avocado
- 1 Tablespoon of organic extra virgin olive oil
- 1 medium organic tomato (chopped)
- 2 Tablespoons of filtered or better still spring water

Directions:

First you make the dressing by:

1. Adding the lemon juice, sea salt, avocado, water, and cilantro to a small blender of Magic Bullet.
2. After which you blend until smooth, adding more water if necessary; set aside.
3. At this point, you divide the lettuce between plates.
4. Then you top with black beans and tomatoes.
5. Finally, you drizzle with dressing and serve.

Dill Salmon Salad Over Spring Mix Recipe

Serves: 2

Ingredients

- 6 cups of Earthbound Farm Organic Spring Mix
- 4 Tablespoons of organic lemon juice
- ¼ teaspoon of organic dill weed (dried)
- 8 organic cherry tomatoes
- ¼ medium organic red onion (finely chopped)
- 1 teaspoon of organic dry mustard
- 1 pinch of Celtic sea salt
- ¼ teaspoon of freshly ground black pepper
- 2 cans of Wild Planet Sockeye Salmon

Directions:

1. First, you add mustard, salt, lemon juice, olive oil and pepper to a small bowl.
2. After which you whisk well and set aside.
3. After that, you drain salmon and add to a medium bowl.
4. Then you add the onions and dill to the salmon.
5. Stir well to combine as you arrange spring mix on plates.
6. At this point, you top with equal portions of salmon mixture.
7. Finally, you place four cherry tomatoes on each salad.
8. Then you drizzle with dressing and serve.

Shrimp Caesar Salad Recipe

Serves: 4

Ingredients

- 2 Tablespoons of organic extra virgin olive oil
- 2 teaspoon of organic Dijon mustard
- A clove of organic garlic (coarsely chopped)
- A pound of wild shrimp
- 4 oz. of organic Asiago cheese (grated)
- 3 Tablespoons of organic lemon juice
- 3 whole anchovies (coarsely chopped)
- ½ teaspoon of freshly ground black pepper
- 8 cups of shredded organic romaine lettuce

Directions:

1. You first of all cook the shrimp.
2. After which you bring a pot of filtered water to a boil.
3. After which you add shrimp; cook until tails curls and shrimp turn pink.
4. Then you drain shrimp and chill over ice.
5. At this point, you add mustard, anchovies, lemon juice and garlic to a food processor or Magic Bullet.
6. Furthermore, you process until smooth and with the motor running, gradually add oil; process until creamy.
7. This is when you add ¼ cup Asiago cheese and black pepper; pulse until combined.
8. After that, you peel and devein the shrimp.
9. Then combine romaine and shrimp in a large bowl; add the dressing and toss to coat.

10. Finally, you divide among plates, top with the remaining ¼ cup Asiago cheese.
11. You can now serve.

Arugula, Fig & Gorgonzola Salad Recipe

Serves: 4

Ingredients

      2 oz. of organic gorgonzola cheese

      6 cup of organic arugula

      4 medium organic figs (halved)

Directions:

First, you place arugula on serving dishes.

After which you top each with two fig halves and one-half ounce of cheese.

Then you serve with dressing of choice.

Baby Spinach Salad with Creamy Italian Dressing Recipe

Serves: 4

Ingredients

⅓ medium organic red onion (thinly sliced)

6 cups of fresh organic baby spinach

¼ teaspoon of Celtic sea salt

½ teaspoon of dried basil

1 Tablespoon of organic extra virgin olive oil

¼ teaspoon of dried oregano

⅓ cup of plain organic Greek yogurt

1 Tablespoon of organic apple cider vinegar

¼ teaspoon of freshly ground black pepper

Directions:

1. First, you whisk together the oil, salt, basil yogurt, vinegar, black pepper, and oregano in a small bowl.
2. After which you refrigerate dressing until ready to serve.
3. After that, you place the spinach in a large salad bowl.
4. Then you top with onion.
5. Finally, you drizzle the dressing over the salad and serve.

Thyroid Healing Delectable Salad dressing

Paleo Macadamia Mayonnaise Recipe

Serves: 20

Ingredients

> 2 Tablespoons of fresh lemon juice
>
> 16 Tablespoons of Olivado Macadamia Nut Oil
>
> ½ teaspoon of dry mustard
>
> ¼ teaspoon of Celtic sea salt
>
> 1 large organic egg

Directions:

1. First, you blend lemon juice, egg, mustard powder and salt in a blender, food processor or VitaMix and with blender running constantly, slowly dribble in the oil, a little at a time, until it's thick and creamy.
2. Then you keep refrigerated to make it thicken.

Cherry Balsamic Vinaigrette Recipe

Serves: 12

Ingredients

¼ teaspoon of Celtic sea salt

¼ teaspoon of freshly ground black pepper

½ cup of organic balsamic vinegar

¼ cup of Cascadian Farm Organic Cherries Cascadian Farms Organic Cherries

¼ cup of organic extra virgin olive oil

Directions:

1. First, you add cherries to a small saucepan with 2 Tablespoons of purified or spring water.
2. After which you heat over medium heat and bring cherries to a gentle simmer.
3. After that, you transfer cherries to Magic Bullet with balsamic vinegar, salt and pepper.
4. Then you pulse to puree to a smooth consistency.
5. At this point, you add oil and pulse again for another 20 seconds to combine, adding water to thin, if necessary.
6. Finally, you keep refrigerated in an airtight container for up to 1 week.

Buttermilk Ranch Dressing Recipe

Serves: 16

Ingredients

- 4 Tablespoons of Wilderness Family Naturals Mayonnaise Wilderness Family Naturals Coconut Mayonnaise
- 2 Tablespoons of organic apple cider vinegar
- 3 Tablespoons of chopped fresh chives (chopped)
- ½ teaspoon of garlic powder
- ½ cup of organic buttermilk
- ½ teaspoon of Celtic sea salt
- ½ teaspoon of freshly ground black pepper

Directions:

1. First, you whisk mayonnaise, garlic, buttermilk, vinegar, salt and pepper in a small bowl until smooth.
2. After which you stir in herbs.
3. Then you keep refrigerated for up to one week.

Tomato Mayonnaise (Vinegar Free) Recipe

Serves: 20

Ingredients

- 1 large organic egg
- ½ teaspoon of Celtic sea salt
- ½ medium organic tomato (peeled and seeded)
- ¾ cup of organic extra virgin olive oil
- ¼ teaspoon of mustard powder
- 2 Tablespoons of minced basil
- 1 Tablespoon of organic lemon juice

Directions:

1. First, you add egg, lemon, salt and mustard to a food processor and blend.
2. After which you add oil in a slow steady stream until it is fully blended.
3. After that, you chop tomato pulp and add to food processor with the basil.
4. Then you blend for about 30 seconds.
5. Make sure you keep refrigerated.

Basic Vinegar-Free Salad Dressing Recipe
Serves: 16
Ingredients

- 8 Tablespoons of organic extra virgin olive oil
- ¼ teaspoon of freshly ground black pepper
- 1 teaspoon of Celtic sea salt
- 1 teaspoon of dry mustard
- 4 Tablespoons of organic lemon juice

Directions:

1. First, you blend all ingredients together in a small bowl or cruet.
2. Then you keep refrigerated.

CONCLUSION:

It time for you to take control of your health with these diet recipes and become a true thyroid expert.

www.ingramcontent.com/pod-product-compliance
Lightning Source LLC
Chambersburg PA
CBHW081723100526
44591CB00016B/2483